EXPLANATORY NOTES

FINANCIAL SERVICES AND MARKETS ACT 2000

GRANGIS UK Publishing

Adapted and published by GRANGIS (Grand Register Library).
Online: www.grangis.com
E-mail: contact@grangis.com

In this version:
ISBN: 979-8-88559-036-5

Note: This is the original version (as it was originally enacted). Title, sub-title and the generated date is as marked on the pages.

These notes refer to the Financial Services and Markets Act 2000 (c.8)

EXPLANATORY NOTES

FINANCIAL SERVICES AND MARKETS ACT 2000

PART VII: CONTROL OF BUSINESS TRANSFERS

Section 107: Sanction of the court for business transfer schemes

Section 112: Effect of order sanctioning business transfer scheme

Section 113: Appointment of actuary in relation to reduction of benefits

Section 114: Rights of certain policyholders

Section 115: Certificate for the purpose of insurance business transfers overseas

Section 116: Effect of insurance business transfers authorised in other EEA States

Section 117: Power to modify this Part

PART VIII: PENALTIES FOR MARKET ABUSE

Section 118: Market abuse

Section 119: The code

Section 120: Provisions included in the Authority's code by reference to the City Code

Section 122: Effect of the code

Section 123: Power to impose penalties in cases of market abuse

Section 124: Statement of policy

Section 128: Suspension of investigations

Section 129: Power of court to impose penalty in cases of market abuse

Section 130: Guidance

PART IX: HEARINGS AND APPEALS

Section 132: The Financial Services and Markets Tribunal

Section 133: Proceedings: general provision

Section 134: Legal assistance scheme

Section 135: Provisions of the legal assistance scheme

Section 136: Funding of the legal assistance scheme

Section 137: Appeal on a point of law

PART X: RULES AND GUIDANCE

Chapter I: Rule-Making Powers

Section 138: General rule-making power

Section 139: Miscellaneous ancillary matters

Section 141: Insurance business rules

Section 256: Requests for revocation of authorisation order

Section 257: Directions

Section 258: Applications to the court

Section 259: Procedure in giving directions under section 257 and varying them on Authority's own initiative

Section 260: Procedure: refusal to revoke or vary direction

Section 261: Procedure: revocation of direction and grant of request for variation

Chapter IV: Open-ended investment companies

Section 262: Open-ended investment companies

Section 263: Amendment of section 716 Companies Act 1985

Chapter V: Recognised overseas schemes

Section 264: Schemes constituted in other EEA States

Section 265: Representations and references to the Tribunal

Section 266: Disapplication of rules

Section 267: Power of authority to suspend promotion of scheme

Section 268: Procedure in giving directions under section 267 and varying them on Authority's own initiative

Section 269: Procedure on application for variation or revocation of direction

Section 270: Schemes authorised in designated countries or territories

Section 271: Procedure

Section 272: Individually recognised overseas schemes

Section 273: Matters that may be taken into account

Section 274: Applications for recognition of individual schemes

Section 275: Determination of applications

Section 276: Procedure when refusing an application

Section 277: Alteration of schemes and changes of operator, trustee or depository

Section 278: Rules as to scheme particulars

Section 279: Revocation of recognition

Section 280: Procedure

Section 332: Rules in relation to persons to whom the general prohibition does not apply

Section 333: False claims to be a person to whom the general prohibition does not apply

PART XXI: MUTUAL SOCIETIES

PART XXII: AUDITORS AND ACTUARIES

Section 340: Appointment

Section 342: Information given by auditor or actuary to the Authority

Section 343: Information given by auditor or actuary to the Authority: persons with close links

Section 344: Duty of auditor or actuary resigning etc. to give notice

Section 345: Disqualification

Section 346: Provision of false or misleading information to auditor or actuary

PART XXIII: PUBLIC RECORD, DISCLOSURE OF INFORMATION AND CO-OPERATION

Section 347: The record of authorised persons etc.

Section 348: Restrictions on disclosure of confidential information by Authority etc.

Section 349: Exceptions from section 348

Section 350: Disclosure of information by the Inland Revenue

Section 350: Competition information

Section 352: Offences

Section 353: Removal of other restrictions on disclosure

Section 354: Authority's duty to cooperate with others

PART XXIV: INSOLVENCY

Voluntary arrangements

Section 356: Authority's powers to participate in proceedings: company voluntary arrangements

Section 357: Authority's powers to participate in proceedings: individual voluntary arrangements

Section 358: Authority's powers to participate in proceedings: trust deeds for creditors in Scotland

Administration orders

Section 359: Petitions

Section 360: Insurers

Section 362: Authority's powers to participate in proceedings

Receivership

Section 363: Authority's powers to participate in proceedings

Voluntary winding up

Section 365: Authority's powers to participate in proceedings

Section 366: Insurers carrying on long-term business

Winding up by the court

Section 367: Winding-up petitions

Section 368: Winding-up petitions: EEA and Treaty firms

Section 371: Authority's powers to participate in proceedings

Bankruptcy

Section 372: Petitions

Section 374: Authority's powers to participate in proceedings

Provisions against debt avoidance

Section 375: Authority's right to apply for an order

Supplemental provisions concerning insurers

Section 376: Continuation of contracts of long-term insurance where insurer in liquidation

Section 377: Reducing the value of contracts instead of winding up

Section 378: Treatment of assets on winding up

Section 379: Winding-up rules

PART XXV: INJUNCTIONS AND RESTITUTION

Section 380: Injunctions

Section 381: Injunctions in cases of market abuse

Section 382: Restitution orders

Section 383: Restitution orders in cases of market abuse

Section 384: Power of Authority to require restitution

PART XXVI: NOTICES

PART XXVII: OFFENCES

PART XXVIII: MISCELLANEOUS

Reciprocity powers

Section 411: Tax treatment of levies and repayments

Section 412: Gaming contracts

Section 413: Protected items

Section 414: Service of notices

Section 415: Jurisdiction in civil proceedings

Section 416: Provisions relating to industrial assurance and certain other enactments

PART XXIX: INTERPRETATION

Section 418: Carrying on regulated activities in the United Kingdom

Section 419: Carrying on regulated activities by way of business

Section 420: Parent and subsidiary undertaking

PART XXX: SUPPLEMENTAL

Section 426: Consequential and supplementary provision

Section 427: Transitional provisions

Section 429: Parliamentary control of statutory instruments

Schedule 1: the Financial Services Authority

PART I: GENERAL

Paragraph 2: Constitution

Paragraph 3: Non-executive members of the governing body

Paragraph 4: Functions of the non-executive committee

Paragraph 5: Arrangements for discharging functions

Paragraph 6: Monitoring and enforcement

Paragraph 7: Arrangements for the investigation of complaints

Paragraph 8: Investigation of complaints

Paragraph 9: Records

Paragraph 10: Annual report

Paragraph 11: Annual public meeting

PART II: STATUS

Paragraphs 14 and 15: Exemption from requirement of "limited" in Authority's name

These notes refer to the Financial Services and Markets Act 2000 (c.8) which received Royal Assent on 14 June 2000

FINANCIAL SERVICES AND MARKETS ACT 2000

EXPLANATORY NOTES

INTRODUCTION

1. These explanatory notes relate to the Financial Services and Markets Act 2000 ("the Act") which received Royal Assent on 14 June 2000. They have been prepared by HM Treasury in order to assist the reader in understanding the Act. They do not form part of the Act and have not been endorsed by Parliament.

2. The notes need to be read in conjunction with the Act. They are not, and are not meant to be, a comprehensive description of the Act. So where a section or part of a section does not seem to require any explanation or comment, none is given.

SUMMARY

3. The Act provides the framework within which a single regulator for the financial services industry, the Financial Services Authority ("the Authority"), will operate. It equips the Authority with a full range of statutory powers and creates the Financial Services and Markets Tribunal ("the Tribunal"). The Act also establishes the framework for single ombudsman and compensation schemes to provide further protection for consumers.

4. The Act makes provision, amongst other things, with respect to:

- the constitution and accountability of the Authority;
- the definition of the scope of regulated activities;
- the control of financial promotion;
- powers of the Authority to authorise, regulate, investigate and discipline authorised persons;
- the recognition of investment exchanges and clearing houses;
- arrangements for the approval of controllers and the performance of regulated activities;
- the oversight of financial services provided by members of the professions;
- regulation and marketing of collective investment schemes;
- certain criminal offences;
- powers to impose penalties for market abuse; and
- the transfer to the Authority of registration functions in respect of building societies, friendly societies, industrial and provident societies and certain other mutual societies.

5. An overview of the Act is set out below. A detailed description of each Part and the sections is contained in the commentary. Terms used are defined in the text where they first appear. There is a glossary of certain terms defined in the Act and certain other terms which are used throughout these notes.

BACKGROUND

Financial Services Overview

6. The UK financial services industry accounts for approximately 7 per cent of GDP, employing over 1 million people in the City of London and across the country.

7. Businesses to be authorised and regulated under the Act include:

- Banks
- Building societies
- Insurance companies
- Friendly societies
- Credit unions
- Lloyd's
- Investment and pensions advisers
- Stockbrokers
- Professional firms offering certain types of investment services
- Fund managers
- Derivatives traders

Regulatory Framework

8. The regulation of financial services has, historically, been the responsibility of a range of different bodies:

- the Authority (formerly the Securities and Investment Board);
- the Self-Regulating Organisations ("SROs"): most recently the Personal Investment Authority, the Investment Management Regulatory Organisation and the Securities and Futures Authority;
- the former Supervision and Surveillance Branch of the Bank of England;
- the Building Societies Commission;
- the Insurance Directorate of the Treasury;
- the Friendly Societies Commission; and
- the Registry of Friendly Societies.

9. Following the Government's announcement of its proposals to introduce legislation to reform the regulation of financial services in May 1997, steps were taken to transfer responsibility for regulation to the Authority. Certain functions under the Banking Act 1987 ("Banking Act") were transferred by the Bank of England Act 1998. In other cases, the Authority entered into contracts with the relevant bodies to perform regulatory functions on their behalf. For example, the Treasury contracted with the Authority for the performance of certain functions under the Insurance Companies Act 1982 ("ICA 1982"). Many relevant staff transferred to the Authority and relocated to

its headquarters building. This process of integration will be completed when the Act is brought into force.

10. The Act will broadly continue the regime for recognised investment exchanges and clearing houses under the Financial Services Act 1986 ("FS Act 1986"), although the Authority's powers under the Act will be widened as compared with those under the predecessor legislation. The Authority will have powers to regulate the Lloyd's insurance market, and have powers of direction over the Council of Lloyd's, although the latter will retain its responsibilities under Lloyd's Acts for the superintendence and governance of the Society of Lloyd's. The recognised professional bodies regime under the FS Act 1986 will not continue. Professional firms (such as solicitors, accountants and actuaries) carrying on mainstream regulated activities will be authorised and regulated directly by the Authority. However, some categories of professional firm will benefit from an exclusion from the scope of regulation under the Act, subject to arms-length oversight by and certain powers of the Authority. The Act does not affect the professional bodies' wider powers to regulate the professional activities of members of their respective professions.

11. The Act is intended to coordinate and modernise financial regulatory arrangements which are currently established under a number of different enactments:

- the Credit Unions Act 1979
- the Insurance Companies Act 1982
- the Financial Services Act 1986
- the Building Societies Act 1986
- the Banking Act 1987
- the Friendly Societies Act 1992

12. Those enactments are generally supplemented by secondary legislation or rules. It is intended that the powers conferred by section 426 will be used so that the relevant parts of that legislation, and rules and regulations made under it, will be substantially repealed when the Act comes into force. Certain other enactments will also be repealed, or substantially repealed, including the Policyholders Protection Acts 1975-97, the Industrial Assurance Acts 1923-48 and the Insurance Brokers (Registration) Act 1977.

13. The Act also provides for the transfer of the remaining functions, including for example functions relating to the registration of mutual societies, of the Building Societies Commission, the Friendly Societies Commission and the Registry of Friendly Societies.

Consultation and scrutiny

14. In July 1998, the Treasury published a paper entitled *Financial Services and Markets Bill: A Consultation Document* which explained its policy in detail and included a draft of the Bill. That consultation exercise attracted comments from over 220 firms and bodies interested in the regulation of financial services, including those representing consumers. The Treasury also published a number of relevant consultation papers, including drafts of secondary legislation to be made under the Act. Copies of relevant documents, including consultation papers and press notices, were made available at the Treasury's website (www.hm-treasury.gov.uk).

15. The draft Bill was subject to pre-legislative scrutiny prior to its introduction into the House of Commons. The Treasury Committee published its third report of Session 1998-1999 on Financial Services Regulation in February 1999 (*Financial Services Regulation, Volumes I and II;* House of Commons 73 I – II). The Government's response was published in March 1999 (*Financial Services Regulation: The Government's Response to the Third Report from the Committee of Session 1998-99;* House of Commons 347).

16. A Joint Committee of both Houses of Parliament was also established to consider aspects of the draft Bill. That committee was also able to consider the Treasury's Progress Report published in March 1999. The Joint Committee published its first report on 29 April 1999 (*Draft Financial Services and Markets Bill: First Report*; House of Lords, 50 I – II; House of Commons, HC328 I – II) and its second report on 2 June 1999 (*Draft Financial Services and Markets Bill: Second Report;* House of Lords, 66; House of Commons, HC465). The Government response to the reports of the Joint Committee on Financial Services and Markets was published in June 1999.

17. The Bill was introduced into the House of Commons on 17 June 1999 and given its second reading on 28 June 1999. The Bill was the first public Bill to be carried over from session of Parliament to the another, under a new procedure recommended by the Select Committee on Modernisation of the House of Commons. The Bill was scrutinised in Standing Committee A between 6 July 1999 and 9 December 1999 (35 sessions). Report Stage took place on 27 January 2000 and on 1 and 9 February 2000. The Bill also received its third reading in the House of Commons on 9 February 2000.

18. The Bill was introduced into the House of Lords on 10 February 2000. It received its second reading on 21 February 2000. There were five Committee days, between 16 and 30 March 2000, followed by three days on Report, on 13 and 18 April 2000 and on 9 May 2000. The Bill received its third reading on 18 May 2000.

19. While the Bill was before the House of Lords, the Treasury also submitted a number of memoranda on the powers to make delegated legislation under the Bill to the Delegated Powers and Deregulation Committee. The Committee reported its view in a number of published reports. The relevant reports were the Seventh Report (16 February 2000), Eighth Report (8 March 2000), Tenth Report (15 March 2000) Twelfth Report (12 April 2000) and Sixteenth Report (17 May 2000). The Treasury's memorandum in each case was annexed to the report.

20. The Bill returned to the Commons for consideration of Lords Amendments on 5 June 2000. It was subsequently returned to the Lords for consideration of Commons amendments on 12 June 2000. This completed the Bill's Parliamentary passage. Royal Assent was given on 14 June 2000.

21. The Authority consults widely on the way it proposes to use its powers and carry out functions under the Act in accordance with the requirements under the Act. Full details of the Authority's consultation papers are available on its website (www.fsa.gov.uk) from where copies of current documents can be downloaded.

INTERPRETATION

22. There are many defined words and expressions in the Act.

23. Most of the definitions are for the purpose only of the section or Schedule in which they are used. So, for example, the three words defined in subsections (13), (14) and (15) of section 21 are defined only for the purposes of that section.

24. Where there is no indication that a definition is intended to apply to a group of provisions, a Part of the Act or the Act as a whole, it applies only for the purposes of the section or Schedule in which it appears.

25. Many of these single-provision definitions are just drafting devices to avoid clumsy repetition which would make an already long Act even longer. For example, in section 38 the word "specified" is used on its own on five occasions. The definition in subsection (4) is there to save repeating the words "in an exemption order" each time it is used.

26. Some of the words and expressions that are defined just for the purposes of the particular provision in which the definition occurs are used (and defined separately) in other

provisions — where they may have a different meaning. For example "consumers" is defined separately for the purposes of sections 5(3), 10(7), 14(5) and 138(7) (the definition in section 10(7) differing from the others).

27. The Act consists of a large number of separate Parts. Where a particular Part deals with a self-contained subject there may be a separate interpretation section within the Part (for example section 193, which deals with the interpretation of Part XIII).

28. For the Act as a whole, Part XXIX contains a group of nine sections which deal with expressions used in a number of provisions and other matters which bear on the interpretation of provisions of the Act.

29. The purpose of this glossary is to provide the reader with a guide to words or expressions which are defined generally and so liable to be met in provisions which do not themselves contain the definition.

Expression	*Where defined (references are to sections, unless otherwise specified)*
appointed representative	39(2)
approved person	64(13)
auditors and actuaries rules	417
Authority	1(1)
authorised person	31(2)
authorisation offence	23(2)
body corporate	417(1)
chief executive	417(1)
collective investment scheme	235
Commission	417(1)
compensation scheme	213(2)
compulsory jurisdiction	226(8)
control of information rules	147(1)
controller	422
director	417(1)
documents	417(1)
EEA authorisation	425(1) and Sch 3, para 6
EEA firm	425(1) and Sch 3, para 5
EEA right	425(1) and Sch 3, para 7
EEA State	425(1) and Sch 3, para 8
exempt person	417(1)
financial promotion rules	417(1)
first banking co-ordination directive	425(1) and Sch 3, para 2(1)
first life insurance directive	425(1) and Sch 3, para 3(2)
first non-life insurance directive	425(1) and Sch 3. Para 3(5)

Expression	*Where defined (references are to sections, unless otherwise specified)*
friendly society	417(1)
general guidance	158(3)
general prohibition	19(2)
general rules	138(2)
group	421
home state authorisation	425(2) and Sch 4, para 1
home state regulator	425(1) and Sch 3, para 9
host state regulator	425(1) and Sch 3, para 11
incorporated friendly society	417(1)
industrial and provident society	417(1)
insurance business rules	141(5)
insurance directives	425(1) and Sch 3, para 3(1)
investment services directive	425(1) and Sch 3, para 4
legal assistance scheme	134(4)
listed securities	14(7)
manager	423
market abuse	118(1)
Minister of the Crown	417(1)
money laundering rules	417(1)
notice of control	178(5)
ombudsman scheme	225(3)
open-ended investment company	236
own initiative power	45(5)
parent undertaking	420
Part IV permission	40(4)
partnership	417(1)
policy	424(2)
prescribed	417(1)
price stabilising rules	417(1)
private company	417(1)
prohibition order	56(2)
recognised clearing house	285
recognised investment exchange	285
recognised scheme	237(3)
registered friendly society	417(1)

Expression	*Where defined (references are to sections, unless otherwise specified)*
regulated activity	22
regulating provisions	159(1)
regulatory objectives	2
regulatory provisions	302(1)
rule	417(1)
rule-making instrument	153
scheme manager	212(1)
scheme operator	225(2)
scheme particulars rules	248(1)
second banking co-ordination directive	425(1) and Sch 3, para 2(2)
second life insurance directive	425(1) and Sch 3, para 3(6)
second non-life insurance directive	425(1) and Sch 3, para 3(3)
seventh company law directive	417(1)
single market directives	425(1) and Sch 3, para 1
subsidiary undertaking	420
supervisory notice	395(13)
third life insurance directive	425(1) and Sch 3, para 3(7)
third non-life insurance directive	425(1) and Sch 3, para 3(4)
threshold conditions	41
Treaty	417(1)
Treaty firm	425(2) and Sch 4, para 1
Tribunal	132(1)
trust scheme rules	247(1)
UK authorised person	178(4)
UK firm	425(1) and Sch 3, para 10
unit trust scheme	237
voluntary jurisdiction	227(12)

Notices

30. The Act frequently refers to the Authority proceeding by way of giving a "warning notice" or a "decision notice". The requirement to proceed in this way has particular procedural consequences, both in terms of the contents of those types of notice and of how action initiated by them must be taken forward. Those consequences are governed by the provisions of Part XXVI of the Act, to which reference should be made whenever the Authority is directed to proceed in this way.

GLOSSARY OF TERMS USED IN THE EXPLANATORY NOTES

31. In addition to the defined terms above, for convenience, these explanatory notes also use certain other abbreviated terms as set out below.

Term used in these notes	*Meaning*
Banking Act	Banking Act 1987
CC Act 1974	Consumer Credit Act 1974
Companies Act	Companies Act 1985
competent authority	the competent authority for listing
DGFT	Director General of Fair Trading
EC directives	Directives adopted by the relevant European Community institution
FS Act 1986	Financial Services Act 1986
ICA 1982	Insurance Companies Act 1982
oeic	open-ended investment company
SROs	Self-Regulating Organisations, which are responsible for the regulation of investment business under the FS Act 1986

THE ACT

32. The Act is in 30 Parts.

Part I, The Regulator. This Part sets out the Authority's general duties and statutory objectives. It also, with Schedule 1, imposes requirements about the Authority's constitution and accountability and about the exercise of certain of its functions.

Part II, Regulated and Prohibited Activities. This Part provides a power for the Treasury to set the scope of regulation by order, within the overall object and purpose of the Act. It prohibits persons who are not authorised (or exempt) from carrying on a regulated activity in the United Kingdom and from holding themselves out as being authorised or exempt. It also sets out arrangements for the regulation of financial promotion.

Part III, Authorisation and Exemption. This Part sets out which persons are to be authorised for the purposes of the Act and gives the Treasury power to exempt certain persons from the requirement to be authorised. Authorised persons will include those persons given permission under Part IV and certain persons from other member States who are authorised in accordance with arrangements under the Treaty of Rome (the "Treaty") and the single market directives.

Part IV, Permission to Carry on Regulated Activities. This Part entitles persons to apply for the Authority's permission to carry on particular regulated activities and makes provision about the giving, variation and revocation of such permissions by the Authority.

Part V, Performance of Regulated Activities. This Part requires persons, such as employees and office holders, who perform specified types of function for authorised persons, to be approved by the Authority. It requires such approved persons to behave in a way that complies with any statements of principle issued by the Authority and gives the Authority certain disciplinary powers. It also gives the Authority powers to prohibit persons from carrying out functions in relation to regulated activities.

Part VI, Official Listing. This Part sets out the powers of the competent authority and the obligations of issuers listed securities. It makes provision for the maintenance of, and admission to, the official list, and for the making of listing rules (including listing rules in relation to sponsors).

Part VII, Control of Business Transfers. This Part creates a mechanism for the transfer of banking and insurance business, subject to a court procedure and regulatory scrutiny.

Part VIII, Penalties for Market Abuse. This Part confers on the Authority power to impose penalties for market abuse. The Act sets out the kinds of behaviour which constitute market abuse and requires the Authority to produce a code which help to determine whether particular behaviour amounts to market abuse.

Part IX, Hearings and Appeals. This Part establishes the Tribunal and sets out the procedure for referring cases to it where the Authority has decided to take regulatory action under the various powers conferred by the Act. It gives a right to appeal against a decision of the Tribunal on a point of law.

Part X, Rules and Guidance. This Part confers powers upon the Authority to set regulatory requirements for persons authorised under the Act. It gives the Authority power to issue guidance on requirements imposed by and under the Act. It also sets out the procedures that the Authority must follow in exercising those powers.

Part XI, Information Gathering and Investigations. This Part sets out the powers of the Authority and of the Secretary of State to require the production of information and documents, to require reports to be prepared, to conduct investigations and to gain access to premises with a warrant.

Part XII, Control over Authorised Persons. This Part requires persons who propose to acquire control over certain authorised persons to notify, and secure the approval of, the Authority.

Part XIII, Incoming Firms: Intervention by the Authority. This Part confers power on the Authority to intervene in the activities of authorised persons from other member States who are authorised in accordance with rights under the Treaty and EC directives. It sets out the grounds on which the power is exercisable and the procedure for exercising it.

Part XIV, Disciplinary Measures. This Part gives the Authority powers to issue public statements about, or impose penalties on, authorised persons who fail to comply with requirements imposed by or under the Act.

Part XV, The Financial Services Compensation Scheme. This Part requires the Authority to create a scheme for the payment of compensation to consumers who suffer financial loss as a consequence of the inability of an authorised person to meet its liabilities. It also confers a certain number of powers on the manager of the scheme.

Part XVI, The Ombudsman Scheme. This Part requires the Authority to establish a single, compulsory ombudsman scheme for the speedy and informal resolution of disputes between members of the public and authorised persons and confers certain powers on the operator of the ombudsman scheme for that purpose. It also provides for the ombudsman to adjudicate on certain other types of dispute, on a voluntary basis.

Part XVII, Collective Investment Schemes. This Part provides for the regulation of collective investment schemes.

Part XVIII, Recognised Investment Exchanges and Clearing Houses. This Part sets out the regulatory regime for investment exchanges and clearing houses and provides for competition scrutiny of the regulatory provisions and practices of those bodies.

Part XIX, Lloyd's. This Part makes the Society of Lloyd's an authorised person and gives the Authority certain powers to direct the affairs of the Society, its members and Lloyd's managing and members' agents. It also provides for the regulation of former underwriting members of the Society.

Part XX, Provision of Financial Services by Members of the Professions. This Part creates an exemption for members of the professions providing financial services to clients in particular circumstances and gives the Authority an oversight role and certain powers in relation to firms that benefit from the exemption.

Part XXI, Mutual Societies. This Part confers powers on the Treasury to transfer to the Authority and to the Treasury certain functions relating to the registration and regulation of building societies, friendly societies and industrial and provident societies and certain other mutual societies. It also confers powers to dissolve certain statutory bodies.

Part XXII, Auditors and Actuaries. This Part concerns the appointment of auditors and actuaries by authorised persons and their responsibilities.

Part XXIII, Public Record and Disclosure of Information. This Part requires the Authority to maintain a public record of authorised (and certain other) persons, and makes provision about the purposes for which confidential information may be disclosed by and to the Authority and other persons having functions under the Act.

Part XXIV, Insolvency. This Part gives the Authority powers to ask the courts to wind up, or initiate other insolvency procedures against, authorised (and certain other) persons. It also enables the Authority to be heard by the court when such proceedings are commenced by third parties.

Part XXV, Injunctions and Restitution. This Part gives the Authority and the Secretary of State powers to seek injunctions in relation to regulatory contraventions and offences for which the Authority has powers to prosecute. It also provides for restitution to be paid to those who have incurred a loss as a result of such a contravention.

Part XXVI, Notices. This Part contains provisions relating to the procedures which the Authority must follow when giving notice of proposed actions under various provisions of the Act. It relates, for example, to decisions not to give permissions or to refuse applications for approvals and to decisions to take regulatory action, such as imposing penalties or making public statements.

Part XXVII, Offences. This Part creates certain offences, including making misleading statements and supplying false information to the Authority. It also makes general provision about offences under the Act and contains provision about the institution of proceedings, for example under Part V of the Criminal Justice Act 1993 (insider dealing) and in relation to money laundering.

Part XXVIII, Miscellaneous. This Part contains provisions giving the Treasury power to direct the Authority and certain other bodies to comply with the UK's international obligations, including European Union decisions to take reciprocal trade action. It also contains provisions concerning gaming contracts, reviews of past business and a number of other matters.

Part XXIX, Interpretation.

Part XXX, Supplemental. This Part contains provisions dealing with the commencement of the legislation and its territorial scope. It confers certain powers on the Treasury in relation to consequential and transitional provisions and with Schedules 18 and 20 to 22 makes certain amendments to other legislation.

COMMENTARY ON SECTIONS

Part I: the Regulator

33. This Part sets out the Authority's general duties and statutory objectives. Together with Schedule 1, it specifies statutory requirements for the Authority's constitution and status and the exercise of certain of its functions. It sets out arrangements which the Authority is required to make for consulting practitioners and consumers. It provides powers for the Treasury to commission reviews of the economy, efficiency and effectiveness with which the Authority has used its resources and to arrange independent inquiries into regulatory matters of serious concern.

Section 1: The Financial Services Authority

34. The Authority is a company limited by guarantee formed under the Companies Act 1985 ("Companies Act") as the Securities and Investment Board for the purpose of carrying out functions under the FS Act 1986. It later assumed functions under the Banking Act and exercised functions under other financial regulatory legislation, including for example under the ICA 1982 on behalf of the Treasury.

Section 2: The Authority's general duties

35. This section requires the Authority to discharge its general functions in accordance with its objectives and with regard to a number of principles. The objectives do not in themselves impose specific statutory duties or functions on the Authority. Rather, the section requires the Authority to carry out its general functions insofar as possible in a way which is compatible with the objectives and which, taking into account any need to balance the objectives as a whole, it considers most appropriate to their fulfilment.

36. *Subsection (2)* lists the Authority's objectives – market confidence, public awareness, the protection of consumers and the reduction of financial crime - which are elaborated in sections 3 to 6.

37. *Subsection (4)* applies those objectives to the Authority's functions in two distinct ways:

- they apply directly to the exercise of the Authority's rule-making, code issuing and general guidance functions taken as a whole;
- they apply to the policy and principles by which it exercises its other functions.

38. *Subsection (3)* lists a number of matters to which the Authority must also have regard in making its rules and guidance and determining the policy and principles by which it exercises its other functions.

Section 5: The protection of consumers

39. *Subsection (2)* sets out factors to which the Authority must have regard when considering the appropriate degree of protection. These are, briefly, the degree of risk involved, the sophistication and experience of the parties to the transaction, the need of customers for advice and information and the general principle that consumers should take responsibility for their decisions. There is no obligation on the Authority to place particular weight on any one of these factors.

*Section 6: **The reduction of financial crime***

40. This provision does not by itself impose any duties on firms. The Authority is expected to pursue this objective in co-operation with various law enforcement agencies.

*Section 7: **Duty of Authority to follow principles of good governance***

41. Part I and Schedule 1 set out, amongst other things, certain requirements of the Authority's constitution. The effect of this section is to require the Authority to have regard, subject to those requirements, to such generally accepted principles of good corporate governance in managing its affairs as it is reasonable to regard as applicable to it. Such principles might include those contained in the Combined Code of the Committee on Corporate Governance. However, some principles, such as relations with shareholders, are not relevant to the Authority as it is a company limited by guarantee and so need not be taken into account.

*Section 8: **The Authority's general duty to consult***

42. This section requires the Authority to make and maintain effective arrangements for consulting practitioners and consumers. These arrangements must include, but are not limited to, the establishment of Practitioner and Consumer Panels. The statutory obligation for the Authority to maintain panels to represent the interests of practitioners and consumers was not present in previous financial services, banking or insurance legislation. The Authority established panels of practitioners and consumers, on a non-statutory basis, before such a requirement was imposed under the Act. The effect of sections 9 and 10 is to require the Authority to continue to maintain those panels.

*Section 11: **Duty to consider representations by the Panels***

43. This section requires the Authority to consider representations made to it by either the Practitioner Panel or the Consumer Panel in accordance with the arrangements under section 8 and, where it disagrees with the views expressed or proposals made in such representations, to give its reasons in writing.

*Section 12: **Reviews***

44. This section enables the Treasury to commission independent reviews of the economy, efficiency and effectiveness with which the Authority has used its resources.

*Section 13: **Right to obtain documents and information***

45. The person appointed by the Treasury to perform a review under section 12 has a right of access to documents held by the Authority.

*Section 14: **Cases in which the Treasury may arrange independent inquiries***

46. This section, together with sections 15 to 18, provides the mechanism for the Treasury to appoint a person to hold an independent inquiry into the circumstances surrounding regulatory events which give rise to serious questions or public concern about the regulatory framework or the effectiveness of regulation in practice. They provide a statutory basis for launching the type of inquiry which has been conducted in the past into the failures of the Bank of Credit & Commerce International ("BCCI") in 1991 and Barings in 1995. The Bingham Inquiry into BCCI was conducted on a non-statutory basis and therefore had no powers to require witnesses to attend or give evidence. The Barings Inquiry was conducted by the Board of Banking Supervision, an advisory body within the Bank of England using powers under the Banking Act.

47. The types of events into which an inquiry may be held are set out in this section. There are two cases. The first case, set out in *subsection (2)*, relates to events concerning persons carrying on regulated activities or collective investment schemes. To trigger

the power, it must appear to the Treasury that two conditions are met. The first of these is that the events posed, or could have posed, a grave risk to the financial system, or caused, or could have caused, significant damage to the interests of consumers. The second condition is that a serious failure in the regulatory system, or in the operation of that system, might have caused or exacerbated the risk or damage, or potential risk or damage.

48. The second case, set out in *subsection (3)*, relates to the listing function under Part VI. Here the Treasury must be concerned with the damage, or potential damage, that might have been caused by a serious failure in the listing regime or its operation.

49. *Subsection (4)* provides that in either case the Treasury may initiate an inquiry only where they consider that it is in the public interest to do so.

*Section 15: **Power to appoint person to hold an inquiry***

50. Under *subsection (1)*, the Treasury may appoint a person whom they consider appropriate to conduct an investigation and, under *subsection (2),* may give directions to that person concerning the scope of the inquiry, how it is to be conducted, when it is to be completed by, and the form of any report of the inquiry. The power to direct the inquiry enables the Treasury to ensure that it focuses on the important questions, and that it is concluded in a manner and on a timescale that is appropriate in light of any public concern there might be.

*Section 16: **Powers of appointed person and procedure***

51. This section gives the person holding the inquiry discretion as to how the inquiry is conducted, and provides that person with powers to obtain evidence, both in the form of documents and through the examination of witnesses. These powers are the same as those exercisable by the High Court, or the Court of Session in Scotland.

*Section 17: **Conclusion of inquiry***

52. This section requires a written report setting out the results of the inquiry and, where appropriate, making recommendations. The Treasury then have discretion whether to publish all or part of the report. However, the Treasury must make sure that they do not publish any material contained in the report which, if published, they consider would seriously prejudice the interests of a particular person, for example because there was a likelihood of subsequent court action in relation to the events covered, or publication would be incompatible with the UK's international obligations, such as those under the confidentiality provisions of one of the single market directives. A copy of any part of the report which is published must be laid before Parliament by the Treasury.

*Section 18: **Obstruction and contempt***

53. The powers of the person appointed to conduct an inquiry are enforceable through certification to the High Court or Court of Session. The person conducting the inquiry must provide the court with a certificate stating the requirement that was imposed and the nature and facts of the alleged failure to comply. The court may then enquire into the matter, hearing witnesses and seeing documents as necessary. If it finds that a person has failed to comply with requirements placed upon him by the person holding the investigation, the court may deal with them as it would with a person in contempt of court.

Part Ii: Regulated and Prohibited Activities

54. This Part provides the mechanism for defining the scope of regulation under the Act and for establishing the extent of the prohibition on issuing unapproved financial promotions.

Section 19: ***The general prohibition***

55. This section contains the basic prohibition on unauthorised persons carrying on regulated activities in the United Kingdom. It is referred to in the Act as "the general prohibition" and prohibits persons who are not authorised or exempt under Part III from carrying on any regulated activity in the United Kingdom. Section 418 elaborates on when regulated activities will be considered to be carried on in the United Kingdom. Contravention of the general prohibition is a criminal offence (see section 23). Agreements made in the course of carrying on an activity in contravention of the general prohibition may be unenforceable (see sections 26, 27 and 29).

Section 20: ***Authorised persons acting without permission***

56. Authorised persons may only carry on in the United Kingdom those regulated activities for which they have been given permission by the Authority under Part IV or by or under any other provision of the Act, for example under Schedule 3, 4 or 5.

57. If an authorised person carries on regulated activities for which he does not have permission the consequences may include any of the sanctions available under Parts IV (Permission to Carry on Regulated Activities), XIII (Incoming Firms: Intervention by Authority) or XIV (Disciplinary Measures). However, if an authorised person acts outside the scope of his permission, he will not commit a criminal offence, and any contract which a person enters into when acting outside the scope of his permission will not be made unenforceable simply by virtue of that fact. *Subsection (3)* permits the Treasury to prescribe cases in which a breach permission gives rise to a right of action for damages.

Section 21: ***Restrictions on financial promotion***

58. This section prohibits unauthorised persons from issuing financial promotions, unless the content of the promotion is approved by an authorised person (who will be subject to rules made by the Authority), or unless an exemption applies. The regulation of financial promotions under the Act is similar to the regulation of investment advertisements and cold-calling under the FS Act 1986. However, section 21 reflects changing technologies and the fact that the borderline between advertisements and unsolicited calls has become blurred. Sections 238 to 241 contain additional provisions relating to the promotion of collective investment schemes.

59. The prohibition applies to "invitations" or "inducements" to engage in investment activity, which are made in the course of business. The Treasury are given power, if necessary, to determine the meaning of "in the course of business". The prohibition will potentially catch communications whether they are made in the United Kingdom, into the United Kingdom from elsewhere, or from the United Kingdom to another country. Communications from outside the United Kingdom can potentially be caught only if they can have an effect in the United Kingdom (*subsection (3)*). It is expected that the exemption order which the Treasury intends to make under *subsection (5)* will further limit the territorial application of the financial promotion regime, so that communications issuing from overseas will generally only be caught if they are directed at the United Kingdom. This will be of particular significance in the context of internet communications.

60. *Subsection (5)* confers a power on the Treasury to make exemptions from the prohibition, similar to the power to make exemptions from the investment advertisement prohibition under the FS Act 1986. It is possible for these exemptions to be made conditional on compliance with rules made by the Authority under section 145.

61. *Subsection (6)* makes clear that the circumstances that can be specified under *subsection (5)* extend to circumstances for which *subsection (3)* expressly makes provision. *Subsection (6)* thus clarifies that an exemption can be made for communications which originate outside the United Kingdom even if they are capable

of having an effect here. *Subsection (6)(a)* and *(b)* deal expressly with the possibility of exemptions for communications originating in specific countries, or specific groups of countries such as EU countries. *Subsection (6)(d)* would allow all communications originating overseas to be exempted if that became appropriate. If such provision were made, *subsection (7)* would allow the Treasury to repeal *subsection (3)*.

62. *Subjections (8) to (12)* govern what constitutes "engaging in investment activity". *Subsections (9) and (10)* give the Treasury power to determine the scope of the prohibition on financial promotion. It is expected that "controlled activities" will be the activities which are regulated under the Act, together with activities which would be regulated, but for an exclusion in an order made under section 22(1). This broad approach reflects the position under the FS Act 1986.

Section 22: ***The classes of activity and categories of investment***

63. This section makes provision as to the classes of regulated activity, if carried on by way of business, and types of investment which are to be regulated under the Act. These are to be prescribed by the Treasury by order to be made under *subsection (1)*. An activity will only be a regulated activity if it is carried on by way of business and is specified in the order under *subsection (1)*. The Treasury will have the power under section 419 to specify circumstances in which an activity shall or shall not be regarded as being carried on by way of business.

64. Schedule 2 indicates the general range of activities and investments that the Treasury may include within the order defining the scope of regulation, but it does not exhaustively list them. It is therefore possible that other activities or investments may be brought within the scope of the regulation under the Act. However, the general nature of the activities set out in Schedule 2 serves as a limitation on the extent of the Treasury's power to bring further activities within the scope of the Act.

Section 23: ***Contravention of the general prohibition***

65. This section makes carrying on a regulated activity in breach of the general prohibition a criminal offence. It is a defence for a person to prove that he exercised due diligence and took all reasonable precautions to avoid committing the offence.

66. A person convicted of this offence, which is referred to as an "authorisation offence", may be subject to a term of imprisonment of up to 2 years if convicted on indictment (6 months on summary conviction) and/or a fine (the current statutory maximum for a fine on summary conviction is £5,000).

Section 24: ***False claims to be authorised or exempt***

67. This creates an offence of falsely describing oneself, or holding oneself out, as authorised or exempt in relation to a particular regulated activity. It is a defence for a person accused of this offence to prove that he exercised due diligence and took all reasonable precautions to avoid committing the offence.

68. Under *subsection (3)* a person found guilty of this offence is liable on summary conviction to a maximum of 6 months imprisonment and/or a fine not exceeding level 5 on the standard scale (currently £5,000). If the offence results from the public display of material, *subsection (4)* permits a fine of up to the statutory maximum (currently £5,000), to be multiplied by the number of days for which any material giving rise to the offence was on public display.

Section 25: ***Contravention of*** *section 21*

69. This section provides that it is an offence to breach the financial promotion prohibition. The sanctions are the same as those which apply under section 23 for a breach of the general prohibition.

70. *Subsection (2)* provides a defence for a person accused of the offence if he can prove either that he believed on reasonable grounds that the content of the communication was prepared or approved by an authorised person, or that he exercised due diligence and took reasonable precautions to avoid committing the offence.

*Section 26: **Agreements made by unauthorised persons***

71. Under this section, agreements concluded in the course of carrying on business in breach of the general prohibition will generally be unenforceable against the customer. However, the customer can still recover any money paid or property transferred and obtain compensation for any loss.

*Section 27: **Agreements made through unauthorised persons***

72. Under this section, agreements made by an authorised person in the course of his authorised business may also be unenforceable by that person if the agreement was entered into as a result of a third party's unauthorised regulated activities. This might arise if, for example, a contract was entered into as a result of investment advice given by an unauthorised third party.

*Section 28: **Agreements made unenforceable by** section 26 **or** 27*

73. This section gives the court discretion to allow the contract which would otherwise be unenforceable under section 26 or 27 to be enforced against the customer. The section also allows for the method by which the amount of compensation which a person may obtain is to be fixed. In order to enforce the contract, the court must be satisfied that it would be "just and equitable" to do so having particular regard to whether:

- where the person contravening the prohibition is a party to the agreement, that he reasonably believed that he had not acted in breach of the prohibition; or
- where the contravention was by a third party, that the authorised person providing the service did not know that the agreement resulted from a contravention.

*Section 29: **Accepting deposits in breach of the general prohibition***

74. This section concerns deposits accepted in contravention of the general prohibition under section 19. If the deposit agreement does not entitle the depositor to immediate repayment on demand, the section provides that the depositor may apply to the court to direct immediate repayment.

75. The court has discretion not to direct repayment if it is satisfied that it would not be just and equitable to direct repayment, having particular regard to whether the deposit-taker reasonably believed that it was not contravening the prohibition.

*Section 30: **Enforceability of agreements resulting from unlawful communications***

76. When a customer enters into an agreement or exercises any rights as a result of a communication in breach of the financial promotion prohibition, the agreement will be unenforceable against him. The customer will also be entitled to recover any property transferred and to receive compensation for losses incurred, but if he chooses to recover property transferred or not to continue the contract, he must return any money received.

77. However, in certain circumstances the courts may enforce agreements made in contravention of the prohibition and allow money and property transferred under the agreement to be retained if it is satisfied that this would be just and equitable, having regard to whether:

- where the person seeking to enforce the agreement was the illegal promoter, that he reasonably believed that the promotion had not been made in breach of the prohibition; or

- where the contravention was by a third party, that the person seeking to enforce it did not know that the agreement resulted from an illegal promotion.

Part Iii: Authorisation and Exemption

78. This Part sets out who is to be authorised and how authorisation is obtained. It also deals with exemptions from the general prohibition for particular persons or classes of persons. The Act provides for a single route to authorisation to operate in the financial services industry, replacing several sector-based regimes.

79. The main route to authorisation is through an application for a permission under Part IV, but authorisation may also be obtained by virtue of:

- notification in accordance with the relevant single market directive from the competent authorities under that directive in another EEA member State. The directives in question are the 2nd Banking Co-ordination Directive for banks and other credit institutions, the Investment Services Directive for investment firms, and the 3rd Life and 3rd Non-life Insurance Directives for insurance companies, including mutual insurers such as friendly societies. The person, who must come from or be incorporated in, or formed under the law of, another member State, is referred to under the Act as an "EEA firm" as defined in Schedule 3;
- exercise, in accordance with Schedule 4, of EU Treaty rights other than or beyond those governed by the single market directives, in which case the person is then referred to in the Act as a "Treaty firm". Again the person must come from, or be incorporated in, or formed under the law of another member State to qualify;
- exercise of rights under the EC directive relating to collective investment undertakings to market in the United Kingdom collective investment schemes or product authorisation of certain open-ended investment companies ("oeics") under regulations to be made under Chapter IV of Part XVII;
- a person being "grandfathered" by virtue of the transitional provisions (see sections 426 and 427). Broadly, the arrangements will cover persons authorised (however described) under the Banking, Financial Services, Insurance, Building Societies, Friendly Societies, Credit Unions and Lloyd's Acts (including members of self-regulating organisations and certain members of recognised professional bodies).

80. The Society of Lloyd's is an authorised purpose by virtue of section 315.

81. It is possible for a person who becomes authorised through one of these routes to carry on regulated activities by virtue of other routes. For instance an EEA firm that is authorised by virtue of its home State notification under a single market directive may extend the range of regulated activities it may carry on through notification under Schedule 4 or an application to the Authority under Part IV for an extension of its permission. A Treaty firm may also obtain additional permission under Part IV.

82. For a person authorised by virtue of having permissions under Part IV, authorisation generally ends when that person no longer has permission to carry on regulated activities, whether at the initiative of the Authority or themselves.

*Section 32: **Partnerships and unincorporated associations***

83. This section makes particular provision for partnerships and unincorporated associations. In principle, it is possible to view a change of partners in a partnership, or a change of the membership of an unincorporated association, as the formation of a new partnership or association. It would be very burdensome and unsatisfactory if such changes meant that a partnership or association that was substantially the same had to renew its authorisation simply because of such a change to its membership. This section therefore ensures that in such circumstances the authorisation is not interrupted. It

also allows the authorisation to pass to a successor partnership or association in the event of dissolution, but only where the members and the business of the successor are substantially the same as the original.

*Section 33: **Withdrawal of authorisation by the Authority***

84. This section requires the Authority to withdraw authorisation from a person who does not have a permission.

*Section 34: **EEA firms***

85. So long as an EEA firm retains its home State authorisation, the Authority may not remove the firm's authorisation under Schedule 3. Such a person will only cease to qualify for authorisation under Schedule 3 if their home State regulator, that is the competent authority under the relevant directive from the person's home State, notifies the Authority that it is withdrawing authorisation for the person to continue to carry on the regulated activities in the United Kingdom, which may or may not be as part of withdrawing the person's authorisation completely, including in the home State.

86. However, if the person has also obtained a permission under Part IV, loss of the grounds for its authorisation under Schedule 3 does not necessarily lead to loss of its authorisation unless the Authority decides that as a result of the changed circumstances it should also withdraw the permission granted by it under Part IV. The Authority may also cancel an authorisation under Schedule 3 if it is requested to do so by the EEA firm.

*Section 35: **Treaty firms***

87. As for an EEA firm, a Treaty firm ceases to qualify for authorisation under Schedule 4 if the relevant home State authorisation is withdrawn. The Authority may remove any additional permission under Part IV, but loss of home State authorisation does not necessarily mean that Part IV permission would be withdrawn. The Authority can also cancel an authorisation on request from a Treaty firm.

*Section 36: **Persons authorised as a result of** paragraph 1(4) **of** Schedule 5*

88. This section enables the Authority to cancel the automatic authorisation under Schedule 5 of managers and depositaries of UCITS schemes at their request. However, if the person also has permissions under Part IV, he does not cease to be an authorised person as a result.

*Section 37: **Exercise of EEA rights by UK firms***

89. Part III of Schedule 3 governs home State regulation by the Authority of UK credit institutions, investment firms and insurance companies exercising their passport rights under the single market directives to establish a branch or provide services in other EEA states.

90. UK firms do not need to be authorised persons in order to exercise EEA passport rights. For example, lending is covered by both the Second Banking Co-ordination directive and the Investment Services Directive. Consequently a firm holding a licence under the Consumer Credit Act 1974 may have an EEA right to carry on Consumer Credit Act business in another EEA state.

*Section 38: **Exemption orders***

91. This section gives the Treasury the power by order to exempt specific natural or legal persons or classes of person from the general prohibition and therefore from the need to be authorised.

92. *Subsection (2)* provides that a person may not benefit from an exemption under an order made under this section if they hold a Part IV permission. However, if they cease to

hold a Part IV permission and the exemption from which they formerly benefited is still extant, they may benefit from it again.

Section 39: Exemption of appointed representatives

93. This section makes an exemption from the general prohibition for appointed representatives of authorised persons. An authorised person cannot be an appointed representative. The exemption only applies if the authorised person, referred to as the principal, has:

- contracted with the representative for the latter to carry on the relevant sort of investment business on their behalf; and
- accepted responsibility in writing for the conduct of those regulated activities.

94. Any regulated activities which are carried on by the representative in accordance with such an arrangement are the responsibility of the principal, who must therefore have permission for all the regulated activities they carry on. The Authority may therefore take regulatory action against the principal in respect of anything said or done (or not said or not done) by the representative in carrying on the regulated activities as if they had expressly authorised the action or inaction in question. Such acts or omissions will be taken into account by the Authority in determining whether the principal has breached any rules or requirements under the Act. However, nothing in this section would make the principal liable to prosecution for a criminal offence in place of the representative. The representative may also be subject to the arrangements under Part V.

95. This section is similar to, and replaces, section 44 of the FS Act 1986. The Treasury have the power to limit the types of business that may be carried on under this exemption. The intention is that an order under *subsection (1)* will broadly reproduce the breadth of the provision under the FS Act 1986, except that it will no longer be possible under this section for an appointed representative to be exempt for some activities and authorised for others. Under a single authorisation regime, it would not be appropriate to allow an authorised person to obtain an exemption rather than have their permission extended to cover those additional activities.

96. The Treasury have the power to prescribe further conditions which the contract between the principal and his representative has to meet. The intention is that this power would be used to reproduce the detailed requirements in sections 44(4) and (5) of the FS Act 1986. These are aimed at ensuring that the principal has adequate control over the activities that the appointed representative may carry on for the benefit of, or on behalf of, other providers of investment products to ensure that the exemption is not misused.

Part Iv: Permission to Carry on Regulated Activities

97. This Part governs the way in which a person can obtain permission to carry on regulated activities. It is through obtaining permission that authorisation is generally obtained under section 31(1). However, this route to authorisation does not apply to those EEA firms who qualify for authorisation by virtue of Schedule 3 or those Treaty firms who qualify by virtue of Schedule 4. These provisions only apply to EEA and Treaty firms to the extent that they have obtained additional permissions beyond those that they obtained under those Schedules.

Section 40: Application for permission

98. This sets out the type of person who can be given permission and therefore who can be authorised by this route. Permission can be applied for and granted to individuals, bodies corporate, partnerships and unincorporated associations. In the case of some regulated activities, however, there are specific constraints on the type of person which may be given permission under the threshold conditions in Schedule 6.

99. Permission may cover a number of regulated activities. Permission is only given once, after that it is simply changed. Thus, *subsection (2)* rules out an application for the grant of permission to an authorised person where he already has permission under this Part. Therefore, if a person wishes to carry on additional activities, he would need to apply for a variation of permission under section 44.

Section 41: ***The threshold conditions***

100. This section requires the Authority to satisfy itself in giving or varying a Part IV permission, or imposing or varying any requirement, that the person concerned will satisfy the threshold conditions set out in Schedule 6 in relation to all the regulated activities covered by his permission. However, this does not prevent the Authority from taking such steps in relation to an authorised person as it considers necessary to secure its regulatory objective of the protection of consumers.

Section 42: ***Giving permission***

101. Having received an application for permission, the Authority must consider it in the light of its duty under section 41. The Authority has discretion to grant permission for all the activities applied for, or just some of them.

102. The Authority can also frame the permission it grants so as to cover activities which are wider or narrower than the activities as described in the application, and may thus impose its own limitations on the way in which an activity may be carried on. This allows the Authority to design the permission in order to be satisfied that the threshold conditions are met in circumstances where it would not be satisfied if it granted the permission sought in full. The ability to grant a wider permission than was applied for would enable the Authority, if it so chose, to have standard types of permission that it granted. However, the Act does not require the Authority to operate in this way.

103. If the applicant is exempt for certain regulated activities by virtue of being a recognised investment exchange or a recognised clearing house, or by virtue of membership of a professional body designated under Part XX, his application, and any resulting permission, is not to be regarded as covering those exempt activities. For other exempt persons, an application under this section will be regarded as covering their exempt activities.

Section 43: ***Imposition of requirements***

104. When granting permission, the Authority may impose what it considers to be appropriate requirements. Such requirements might include requirements on the authorised person to act, or refrain from acting, in a certain way. *Subsection (5)* allows the Authority to specify a period during which such requirements have effect. Thus the Authority might impose a limit on the amount of a certain type of business the person may conduct during the first five years after receiving the permission. This would enable the Authority to continue the current practice adopted by the insurance supervisors of restricting the premium income that can be received by an insurer in the period following its authorisation to undertake a new form of insurance business.

105. Under *subsection (3)*, such requirements may also be imposed in respect of unregulated activities. For instance, the Authority might have misgivings about the way in which a regulated activity might be carried on in conjunction with an unregulated activity that the person already carries on, or which he proposes to carry on. Those misgivings may not justify preventing the person from commencing the regulated activity because the Authority may not consider that the unregulated activity, of itself, casts doubt about the person's fitness to carry on the regulated one. It may, however, be concerned that the juxtaposition of the two activities could be confusing to consumers, or that the manner in which the unregulated activity was carried on might pose a threat to their interests. Therefore, the Authority could place limitations on the way in which the unregulated activity was carried on for a period after the granting of the new permission

in order that it could observe how the activities were carried on, or related to each other, in practice. *Subsection (4)* enables the Authority to take account of the person's membership of a wider group (as defined in section 421).

*Section 44: **Variation etc at request of authorised person***

106. The Authority may vary the permission, including cancelling it completely, at the request of the authorised person, subject to being satisfied that the person will satisfy the threshold conditions for any resulting permission in accordance with section 41. If it is not satisfied, it may refuse the request outright, grant a more limited permission than the one requested, or grant the requested permission, but subject to new requirements. The Authority may also refuse to grant a request for variation on the grounds that refusal is in the interests of consumers or potential consumers.

107. If as a result of the variation, the authorised person would no longer have permission to carry on any regulated activity, the Authority must consider whether it is still necessary for the person to hold a permission at all (and therefore continue to be an authorised person). If it is not necessary, the Authority should cancel the permission.

*Section 45: **Variation etc on the Authority's own initiative***

108. This section gives the Authority the power to revoke or vary the terms of an authorised person's permission on its own initiative (referred to as its "own initiative power"). The power is exercisable on three grounds. These are where it appears to the Authority that:

- the person is failing, or likely to fail, to meet the threshold conditions in relation to the existing permission;
- the person has failed to make use of the permission to carry on a particular regulated activity for a year or more;
- it is desirable to do so in order to protect the interests of consumers or potential consumers.

109. As with the previous section, if as a result of the variation the authorised person no longer has permission to carry on any regulated activity, the Authority must consider whether it is necessary for that person to continue to hold a permission and be an authorised person. If it is not necessary, the Authority should cancel the permission.

*Section 46: **Variation of permission on acquisition of control***

110. The Authority may also impose a new requirement or vary an existing one if:

- someone "acquires control" over the UK authorised person within the meaning of Part XII; and
- the result is that although the Authority does not consider that it has grounds to object to the acquisition, it nevertheless considers that there is some significant uncertainty about the impact of the acquisition, or further acquisition, of control on the conduct of the authorised person's business.

*Section 47: **Exercise of power in support of overseas regulator***

111. This section enables the Authority to cancel or vary a permission on its own initiative on behalf of an overseas regulatory authority. The section gives the Treasury power to prescribe by regulations the sort of overseas authority that the Authority to help. The functions that it is proposed should be prescribed in this way are functions corresponding to those of:

- the Authority itself under this Act;
- the competent authority for listing;

- the Secretary of State under the Companies Act; and
- the prosecuting authorities for insider dealing and money laundering.

112. However, even where the overseas regulator and the provisions they are seeking to enforce meet these requirements, the Authority is not obliged to act in accordance with the request. The Authority must act reasonably, as it must in discharging any of its functions, but it is also directed to consider certain factors in particular. First among these is whether EC law obliges the Authority, as the competent authority under one of the single market directives or otherwise, to assist the overseas authority. Unless there is an EC obligation to act the Authority must consider the further factors listed in *subsection (4)* which include the seriousness of the case and the public interest. The Authority is also able to charge a contribution towards the costs of taking the enforcement action, and to make this a condition of exercising the power. (*Note*: The reference to *subsection (4)* in the definition of "request" in *subsection (7)* is an error. It should only refer to *subsection (5)*.)

Section 48: Prohibitions and restrictions

113. Among the requirements which the Authority can impose on an authorised person when acting under this Part are:

- restrictions on the use or disposal of the authorised person's assets; or
- requirements to transfer its assets or assets it holds on behalf of investors to a trustee approved by the Authority.

114. The purpose of these types of restriction is to prevent an authorised person disposing of particular assets or making certain types of investment, in circumstances where the Authority is concerned about a person's solvency or where it wishes to investigate suspected fraudulent behaviour.

115. Where an authorised person's assets are held by a third party, for example by a bank, *subsection (4)* enables the Authority to give the institution notice of any restrictions it has placed on the authorised person's assets. This notice might state, for example, that a bank should not allow any payments to be made from the authorised person's account without the permission of the Authority. *Subsection (5)(a)* provides that if the institution refuses to comply with a request to make a payment from the account of an authorised person who is subject to a restriction notice, it is not to be taken as a breach of its contract with the authorised person. However, if the institution were to allow a payment to be made from such an account, in breach of a restriction, under *subsection (5)(b)* it would be liable to pay the same amount of money to the Authority.

116. *Subsections (6)* to *(11)* are concerned with the transfer of an authorised person's assets to a trustee approved by the Authority.

117. *Subsection (6)* requires a trustee not to deal with or release any of the assets transferred to them unless the Authority agrees. If the trustee does release assets without the Authority's consent, he is guilty of an offence under *subsection (9)*. However *subsection (11)* protects the position of the persons who are beneficiaries of the trust by preserving all the remedies they would normally have under trust law. The beneficiaries of the trust are the owners of the assets transferred to the trustee. This will be either the authorised person or, where the assets transferred include assets the authorised person was holding or controlling on behalf of other investors, those investors.

118. *Subsection (7)* makes void any charge that the authorised person makes over his assets while they are held by a trustee. Any charges arranged before the assets were transferred to a trustee remain valid. The effect of this is that were the authorised person to enter into a contractual arrangement which gave a third person a right ahead of existing creditors or a liquidator to any of his assets which, as a result of a requirement made

by the Authority under *subsection (3)(b)*, were held by a trustee, that contract would be void and the rights of the liquidator and existing creditors to the assets would be upheld.

Section 49: Persons connected with an applicant

119. *Subsection (1)* of this section makes it clear that, in deciding whether to approve an application for permission, the Authority may also have regard to other relevant persons who are related to the applicant in some way. What constitutes a relevant relationship is not defined, but is left to the Authority to interpret in the particular circumstances of the case.

120. The Authority is obliged under*subsection (2)* to consult with the home State regulator of an EEA firm before granting an application from a person who is a subsidiary undertaking of that firm or the subsidiary undertaking of a parent undertaking of that firm.

Section 50: Authority's duty to consider other permissions etc.

121. An EEA firm, Treaty firm or recognised collective investment scheme may have a Part IV permission in addition to a permission as such a firm or scheme. In considering the exercise of its own initiative power in relation to such an additional permission, the Authority must take account of the relevant EC law and of the home State authorisation of the person concerned. Such consideration may inform the Authority's view on whether the firm or scheme is fit and proper to continue to hold the additional permissions in question, or its view on whether the cancellation or variation it proposes is appropriate in light of the wider assessment of the firm which the home State regulator is responsible for making.

Section 51: Applications under this Part

122. This section sets out the minimum information that must be included in an application for a permission. It also enables the Authority to specify the manner in which an application may be made, for example whether applications by e-mail will be accepted, and such other things that should be included as the Authority considers necessary or appropriate. The Authority can require additional information after the application is received, and can require the applicant to verify any of the information supplied.

Section 52: Determination of applications

123. The Authority is required to determine an application within 6 months of receiving the completed application. The Authority has discretion whether to determine incomplete applications, but it must determine even incomplete applications within 12 months of the initial receipt of the application. The Authority may, of course, refuse an application on the grounds that it is incomplete where it is appropriate to do so. Under *subsection (3)* an applicant may withdraw an undetermined application at any time.

124. Once the Authority has determined an application it must give written notice of its decision and, if the application to be granted, the date upon which the authorisation takes effect and from which the relevant activities may commence. If the Authority proposes to refuse all or part of the application, or impose an additional requirement, it must proceed by way of a warning and decision notice.

Section 53: Exercise of own initiative power: procedure

125. This section set out the procedure the Authority must follow when it proposes to exercise its own-initiative power to vary an authorised person's Part IV permission. If, having regard to the ground on which it is exercising the power, the Authority considers it necessary, the variation may take effect immediately or on a specified date. If no date is specified in this way the variation will take effect only after the time for referring the matter to the Tribunal has expired and any reference (and further appeal) has been

finally determined (see the definition of "open to review" in section 391(8)). The Authority must give the authorised person a written notice which gives the details of the variation, the date on which it takes effect, the reasons for the imposing the variation and for the choice of date. The notice must also inform the person of his right to make representations to the Authority within a specified period, and to refer the matter to the Tribunal.

126. *Subsections (7) to (10)* require the Authority to give further written notice of its response to any representations which are made. This can be a decision not to proceed with the variation (or to cancel it if it has already taken effect), to propose a different variation (in which case the original notice procedure must be repeated), or to proceed with the variation (in which case the person concerned has a further right to refer the matter to the Tribunal).

Section 54: Cancellation of Part IV permission: procedure

127. This section requires the Authority to serve warning and decision notices when cancelling a Part IV permission on its own initiative, under section 45. Warning and decision notices given under this section also attract the rights set out in sections 393 and 394 by virtue of section 392.

Section 55: Right to refer matters to the Tribunal

128. This section confers a right to refer to the Tribunal a decision of the Authority to vary or cancel a permission on its own initiative. It also applies to decisions of the Authority in relation to applications under Part IV, such as a decision to refuse an applications for permission, to impose conditions or to vary a permission other than in the way requested.

Part V: Performance of Regulated Activities

129. This Part confers on the Authority a range of powers which will enable it to ensure that people who work for authorised persons for certain purposes are fit and proper to perform the functions for which they have been engaged. While the focus of regulation is on authorised firms, the Part gives the regulator powers to prevent harm which might otherwise be caused by persons attached to firms.

130. Under the preceding regulatory framework, there is considerable variation between the arrangements applying to employees working in different sectors. The SROs have introduced a contractual system which requires employees to sign up to regulatory and disciplinary arrangements. Lloyd's has applied similar regulation to employees of underwriting agents, using its byelaw making powers. Banking and insurance legislation provides for pre-vetting of certain senior management positions, in some cases as part of the regime for the regulation of controllers of such firms. That legislation does not provide for the regulator to take disciplinary action against those managers, although senior managers, as officers of the firm, could commit a criminal offence where the firm itself had committed such an offence. There is, in addition to the vetting arrangements, a power in section 59 of the FS Act 1986 for the Authority to prohibit a person's employment in connection with investment business. The above arrangements will be replaced by arrangements under this Part.

131. The Part seeks to harmonise these arrangements. It provides a power for the Authority to ban unfit individuals from carrying out specified functions within the financial services sector. It also provides for:

- the Authority to require its approval to be obtained before a person may perform specified functions;
- the Authority to issue statements of principle with which approved persons must comply, and codes of conduct elaborating on the statements; and

- a disciplinary regime for those who fail to comply with the statements of principle.

132. This Part provides for firms and individuals concerned to refer matters to the Tribunal if the Authority proposes to:

- issue a prohibition order;
- refuse an application to vary or revoke a prohibition order;
- refuse an application for approval;
- take disciplinary action; or
- withdraw approval.

133. The Part is primarily directed at the employees of authorised firms. However, it extends beyond employees to include, for example, directors, representatives and contractors of an authorised person, and extends to bodies corporate where relevant. If, for example, a life insurance company entered into a marketing agreement with a firm of estate agents to sell life insurance, the agency and relevant sales staff giving investment advice might need prior approval. Part V would also cover "matrix managers" who carry out certain functions, often on a fairly informal basis, for a group of companies even though technically they are "employees" of a sister company rather than of the authorised person for whom they carry out relevant functions. Such arrangements are increasingly common in multi-national groups.

*Section 56: **Prohibition orders***

134. This section enables the Authority to make an order prohibiting any individual whom it considers is not fit and proper to perform functions in connection with regulated activities. A prohibition may relate to all functions in relation to any regulated activities carried on by all authorised (or exempt) persons or it can specify the kind of functions, activities or authorised (or exempt) persons to which it relates. A prohibition order may be varied or revoked.

135. *Subsection (4)* makes it an offence for an individual not to comply with a prohibition order. The maximum penalty for this offence is a fine at level 5 on the standard scale (currently £5,000). There is, however, a defence under *subsection (5)* for a person who can show that he took all reasonable precautions and exercised all due diligence to avoid committing the offence.

136. *Subsection (6)* imposes an obligation on an authorised person to take reasonable care not to engage individuals who have been disqualified under this section from performing relevant functions. Failure to comply with this requirement could trigger the use of the Authority's powers to amend the authorised person's permission or discipline the firm. It also potentially gives rise to a cause of action under section 71 from a private person who suffers a loss as a consequence of the breach.

137. *Subsection (8)* enables a prohibition order to be issued preventing an individual from performing functions in relation to a regulated activity carried on by an exempt person or a person to whom section 327(1) applies, that is by members of a profession or persons controlled or managed by members of a profession, who benefit from the exemption from the general prohibition under Part XX.

*Section 59: **Approval for particular arrangements***

138. This section requires authorised persons to take reasonable care not to allow persons, natural or corporate, to perform certain functions without the approval of the Authority. *Subsection (2)* similarly requires an authorised person to take reasonable steps to ensure that any contractor does not allow a person to perform such functions without the approval of the Authority. A person in respect of whom approval is given is

an "approved person". The nature of the functions requiring approval will be specified by the Authority's rules, within the limits set out in *subsections (5)* to *(7)* and subject to the normal consultation requirements under Part X. The limits can be summarised:

- The function may enable a person significantly to influence the conduct of the authorised person (for example a director). By virtue of *subsection (9)* account may be taken of influence which might result from a failure properly to carry out that function (for example a proprietary trader).
- The function involves dealing with customers (for example a financial adviser) or dealing with their property (such as a stockbroker) in a way that is substantially connected with the carrying on of a regulated activity by the firm.

139. *Subsection (8)* limits the application of this section in the case of EEA or Treaty firms. The Authority will only have powers to act in relation to functions over which it, rather than the home State regulator, has jurisdiction.

*Section 60: **Applications for approval***

140. This section requires an application for approval to be submitted by the authorised person concerned or, in the case of new firms awaiting authorisation, a prospective authorised person.

141. *Subsection (2)* gives the Authority the powers to specify the information it will require to support applications for different types of posts and *subsection (3)* enables it to request any additional information it needs to assess the suitability of each candidate.

*Section 61: **Determination of applications***

142. This section sets out the basis on which the Authority is to assess the suitability of a candidate for approval, whether they are an individual or a body corporate. *Subsection (1)* requires the Authority to be satisfied that a candidate is fit and proper to perform the functions in question before it is able to give its approval. Where the Authority proposes to refuse an application, section 62 requires it to give a warning and decision notice. Notice must be given to the authorised person, the candidate and, where relevant, a contractor.

*Section 63: **Withdrawal of approval***

143. This section gives the Authority power to withdraw the approval granted for the purposes of section 59 where it no longer considers that the person is a fit and proper person to carry out the functions for which they had been approved, for example because the Authority had obtained new information which cast doubt over its initial assessment.

*Section 64: **Conduct: statements and code***

144. This section gives the Authority power, as part of its wider rule-making functions, to issue statements of principle, setting out in general terms the kinds of behaviour which it requires from approved persons in respect of any particular type of function. Any statements of principle issued under this section must be elaborated by a code of practice. Such a code would not need to be exhaustive but it would have to illustrate the circumstances in which it would regard a principle as having been complied with, or not complied with, as the case may be. Different statements of principle and codes could be made to apply to employees of different categories. The purpose of requiring a code to elaborate on a statement of principle is to prevent the Authority taking a disciplinary action for an alleged breach of a principle in cases where a person had acted in accordance with the code.

145. *Subsection (8)* makes it clear that failure to comply with a principle does not give a third party grounds for action against the approved person. Therefore, if for example a financial adviser employed by an insurance company failed to comply with a statement

of principle when arranging a personal pension, that would not give a customer a right of action against the employee, with whom they had no contractual relationship. This provision would not remove or lessen any rights, including those under contract or by virtue of section 71, the customer may have against the authorised person who had entered into an agreement to provide the pension.

Section 65: Statements and codes: procedure

146. This section sets out the procedure that the Authority is required to follow when issuing a statement or code under section 64. The procedures, including the requirements to consult and publish a cost-benefit analysis, are broadly the same as the procedures that will apply when the Authority exercises other powers to issue codes (for example under section 119) and its rule-making powers under Part X.

Section 66: Disciplinary powers

147. This section gives the Authority a power to take disciplinary action against an approved person when the two conditions set out in *subsection (1)* have been met. The Authority must be satisfied that it is appropriate to take action against him. In this context, the Authority would have to have regard, among other things, to its regulatory objectives set out in Part I. The Authority would need to take into account whether disciplinary action against the approved person, rather than action against the authorised person for whom he works, would be appropriate, taking into account the responsibility of the senior management of the firm for the conduct of the firm and its employees. A second important factor would be to ensure that any action, or any particular course of action, it takes should be proportionate to the nature and seriousness of the misconduct.

148. In addition, the Authority must be satisfied that the person has engaged in misconduct, as defined in *subsection (2)*. One possibility is that the approved person has acted in breach of a statement of principle, issued under section 64, as evidenced by a breach of a code of practice. The other possible situation is that an approved person has been knowingly involved in a breach by the authorised firm of rules made by the Authority or of any requirement imposed by or under the Act.

149. *Subsection (3)* gives the Authority powers to impose a penalty on an approved person or to make a public statement about their misconduct.

150. *Subsection (4)* restricts the period during which the Authority may take action under this section to a period of two years after the Authority became aware of the misconduct. This period reflects the time available to the Secretary of State to bring disqualification proceedings against a company director under the Company Directors Disqualification Act 1986.

Section 69: Statement of policy

151. This section requires the Authority to issue a statement of its policy on the circumstances in which it will impose penalties on approved persons under section 66 and the basis on which the level of penalties will be determined for different types of misconduct. The policy set out in the statement must take into account a number of factors which are set out in *subsection (2)*.

152. *Subsection (8)* requires the Authority to have regard to the statement in force at the time of the misconduct when imposing penalties under this Part.

Section 70: Statements of policy: procedure

153. This section sets out the procedure for issuing a statement of policy under section 69. Before deciding on its policies in these areas, or changing those policies, the Authority will be required to consult the public on its proposals.

Section 71: Actions for damages

154. If a private person suffers a loss because an authorised person has acted in breach of the duty under section 56(6) or 59(1) or (2) (failing to take care to prevent a person carrying out functions in contravention of a prohibition under section 56, or without obtaining the Authority's approval under section 59) he may bring an action for damages against the authorised person (or an exempt person or person to whom clause 327(1) applies in the case of a contravention under section 56(6)). *Subsections (2) and (3)* confer powers on the Treasury, by regulations, to define a "private person" and to specify circumstances in which this section applies to a person other than a private person.

Part Vi: Official Listing

155. EC law requires each member State to nominate or create a competent authority to maintain an official list of securities, to regulate the admission of securities to the Official List, and to monitor issuers' adherence to the listing rules (as explained below) thereafter. In the United Kingdom these functions are exercised by the Authority following the coming into force of the Official Listing of Securities (Change of Competent Authority) Regulations 2000 (SI 2000/968), the competent authority function was exercised by the London Stock Exchange. The provisions of this Part implement these requirements of EC directives. These provisions replace those in Part IV of the FS Act 1986.

156. There is no requirement for issuers of securities, for example companies issuing new shares, to apply for admission to the official list. However, admission to the official list signals that certain standards regarding the financial status and history of the company have been met; that adequate information about a security has been made available to investors at the time of application; and that information about the performance and plans of the issuer will continue to be made available on a continuing basis so long as the company has securities listed on the official list.

157. In carrying out its functions, the competent authority makes rules which govern the admission of securities to listing, the continuing obligations of issuers, the enforcement of those obligations and the suspension and cancellation of listing. These rules are collectively known as "listing rules", which have been published by the competent authority in the "yellow book". The competent authority also has a role in scrutinizing prospectuses and circulars where there is no application for admission to the official list.

Section 72: The competent authority

158. This section confers the functions of competent authority on the Authority. *Subsection (2)* and Schedule 7 make provision for the way in which other provisions of the Act apply to the Authority when exercising functions as the competent authority. However, subsection (3) and Schedule 8 provide a power for the Treasury to transfer some or all of the functions of the competent authority for the United Kingdom to another body.

Section 73: General duty of the competent authority

159. This section sets out the general duties of the competent authority. *Subsection (1)* sets out a number of principles to which the competent authority must have regard in discharging its general functions (as defined in *subsection (2)*).

160. *Subsection (1)* is similar to section 2(3). The requirements of *subsection (1)* are intended to act as constraints on the way the competent authority carries out its functions under Part VI. Unlike section 2(3), this section does not have a principle relating to the responsibilities of senior management. This is because the competent authority is not responsible for the conduct of business or the prudential regulation of listed companies.

Section 74: ***The official list***

161. This section places a duty on the competent authority to continue to maintain the official list. Section 99 allows the competent authority to charge fees for this purpose. Before this Act comes into force, the official list will be made up of securities that have been admitted by the competent authority under the statutory provisions of Part IV of the FS Act 1986 and securities and other financial instruments which were admitted by the competent authority under contract with issuers (for example gilts and covered warrants). Under the Act there will be a single statutory regime for the official listing of all these securities and other instruments.

162. The legislation therefore gives the Treasury a power in *subsection (3)* to provide that certain categories of financial instrument cannot be admitted to the Official List. This is a reserve power to ensure that the Treasury could stop the admission to the list of financial instruments which they consider, for example, pose undue risks to investors. *Subsection (4)* confers powers on the Authority to make listing rules.

Section 75: ***Applications for listing***

163. This section provides that only applications for listing which are by, or with the consent of, the issuer and meet the requirements imposed by the competent authority may be granted. The competent authority can refuse an application for listing where it considers that granting it would be detrimental to the interests of investors.

164. *Subsection (3)* provides that no application for listing can be entertained by the competent authority in respect of securities issued by a body of a prescribed kind. The Treasury intend to use this power to prescribe that securities issued by a private company or by an old public company (within the meaning of section 1 of the Companies Consolidation (Consequential Provisions) Act 1985) cannot be admitted to listing. This will replicate provisions in the FS Act 1986.

Section 77: ***Discontinuance and suspension of listing***

165. Occasionally circumstances arise which mean that normal dealings in listed securities cannot take place. For example, a company may fail to comply with reporting requirements in the listing rules, so that investors and potential investors do not have sufficient information on which to make informed decisions about the company's securities in order to deal in the securities. Alternatively, a company may be in financial difficulties which it has not clarified or quantified. This section gives the competent authority the power to suspend or discontinue the listing of a company's securities in such circumstances. During a suspension, trading in the securities cannot take place on a recognised investment exchange. An issuer may refer a decision to discontinue or suspend listing to the Tribunal.

Section 78: ***Discontinuance and suspension: procedure***

166. This section sets out the procedures to be followed by the competent authority when it suspends or discontinues the listing of any securities under section 77. The procedure is broadly similar to that which applies in the case of other supervisory decisions listed in section 395(13), and which is described in the context of section 53 above.

167. During the procedure for making representations and referring the matter to the Tribunal, it is possible for a suspension or discontinuance to be reversed. If a suspension is cancelled the securities simply remain listed. If a discontinuance is cancelled at this stage, either because the competent authority accedes to representations which are made under *subsection (3)(c)* or because it follows directions of the Tribunal to that effect, *subsection (9)* provides that the securities are regarded as being readmitted to the list as soon as the discontinuance is cancelled and without any fresh admission needing to be granted.

168. *Subsections (10) to (12)* set out a separate procedure which applies, after a suspension has taken effect and after the procedures for making representations and for referring the matter to the Tribunal have been exhausted, if there is a subsequent application for the suspension to be cancelled. In this case the standard warning and decision notice procedure applies as for other applications. However, at this stage in the process, a discontinuance is regarded as final and so there is no procedure for applying for it to be reversed. Instead a fresh application would need to be made for listing under section 75.

Section 79: ***Listing particulars and other documents***

169. Under EC law, where there is an application for the listing of securities which are to be offered to the public in the United Kingdom for the first time, a prospectus must be approved by the competent authority and published. This is provided for by section 84. Where a prospectus is not required, for example because the securities have already been offered to the public or because there is an exemption (as set out in Schedule 11) the competent authority can provide that securities can only be admitted to the official list after publication of listing particulars and other documents approved by the competent authority. Listing particulars are documents which contain information on the nature and circumstances of the applicant and on the securities to be listed. The content is determined by listing rules. The existence of the power will allow investors to make informed decisions about that security.

170. *Subsection (3)* allows the Treasury to prescribe the persons responsible for listing particulars. The Treasury intend to exercise this power to prescribe those persons covered by section 152 of the FS Act 1986. However, the power will allow there to be some flexibility to reflect the admission of any possible types of financial instrument to the official list. This is necessary given the comprehensive nature of the statutory regime under section 74.

Section 80: ***General duty of disclosure in listing particulars***

171. This section places a duty on those responsible for producing listing particulars to ensure that those particulars contain, at the very least, adequate information to enable investors and their professional advisers to make informed decisions about the issuer and securities in question. The competent authority can authorise the omission of certain information in certain circumstances, as set out in section 82.

Section 81: ***Supplementary listing particulars***

172. This section provides that where there is any significant change following the submission of listing particulars to the competent authority but before dealings in the securities have started, supplementary listing particulars must be approved and published.

Section 82: ***Exemptions from disclosure***

173. This section allows the competent authority to authorise the omission of information required by listing rules to be included in listing particulars in certain circumstances. These circumstances are set out in *subsection (1)*; namely, that the disclosure of the information would be contrary to the public interest, would be seriously detrimental to the issuer (for example the disclosure of commercial secrets), or would be unnecessary given the kind of people who could be expected to buy or sell those securities (for example, if the securities were only dealt in by professionals).

174. *Subsection (2)* provides that information cannot be omitted where it would be seriously detrimental to the issuer if that information is essential in order for a person to make an informed assessment. ("Essential information" is defined in *subsection (6)*.)

*Section 83: **Registration of listing particulars***

175. This section requires listing rules to provide that listing particulars must be lodged with the registrar of companies on or before the date on which they are published. The same requirement applies to prospectuses because of section 86. Breach of this requirement is an offence under *subsection (3)*, punishable by a fine..

*Section 84: **Prospectuses***

176. This section provides that a prospectus must be published before securities are offered to the public in the United Kingdom for the first time before admission to the official list. Section 103(6) and Schedule 11 define the circumstances in which a person is to be treated as having offered securities to the public in the United Kingdom. For example, an offer is not regarded as being made, and the requirement to publish a prospectus therefore does not arise, where the offer is made to no more than 50 persons.

*Section 85: **Publication of prospectuses***

177. This section makes it a criminal offence for a person to offer new securities to the public in the United Kingdom before a prospectus has been published. This offence only applies where listing rules require the publication of a prospectus before particular new securities are admitted to the official list.

*Section 87: **Approval of prospectus where no application for listing***

178. Where securities are to be offered to the public in the United Kingdom for the first time and there has been no application for listing, listing rules may allow issuers to submit prospectuses to the competent authority for approval. This section refers to such prospectuses as "non-listing prospectuses". Where such a prospectus has been approved by the competent authority, under EC law it must be recognised by competent authorities in other member States as complying with their own rules on prospectuses. Accordingly, there is no need in these circumstances to obtain further approval from another competent authority if the securities are to be issued in another member State.

*Section 88: **Sponsors***

179. This section enables the competent authority to make listing rules requiring issuers of listed securities, or issuers seeking admission to the list, to appoint a sponsor.

180. *Subsections (2) and (3)* allow the competent authority to approve persons who may act as a sponsor, and to maintain a list of such persons. They also allow the relevant listing rules to specify particular services which must be performed by a sponsor (for example a sponsor might be required to certify that certain requirements for listing are met).

181. *Subsections (4) to (7)* apply the standard warning notice and decision notice procedure where the competent authority proposes to refuse a person's application for approval as a sponsor, or to cancel such approval, and provide the right to refer the matter to the Tribunal where a decision notice is given.

*Section 89: **Public censure of sponsor***

182. This section permits the competent authority to make listing rules which allow it to make public statements to the effect that a sponsor has contravened a requirement imposed on him by the listing rules, subject to the warning and decision notice procedure and a right to refer the matter to the Tribunal. The power to impose financial penalties does not, however, apply to sponsors.

Section 90: Compensation for false or misleading particulars

183. This section provides that a person responsible for listing particulars (or, under this Part as applied by sections 86, 87(5) and Schedule 9, prospectuses or non-listing prospectuses) is liable to pay compensation to those who suffer loss as a result of untrue or misleading statements or the omission of any information which must be contained in those documents. There are some circumstances in which there is no liability to pay compensation. These are set out in Schedule 10.

Section 91: Penalties for breach of listing rules

184. This section gives the competent authority a power to impose financial penalties on issuers who have breached the listing rules. Under the FS Act 1986, the competent authority can issue private or public censures or suspend or cancel the listing of securities. The additional power conferred by this section is intended to provide further flexibility in this area. The competent authority will also be able to impose penalties upon present and former directors (which is defined in section 417 to include shadow directors) who were knowingly involved in a breach of the listing rules. However, it may not impose a penalty later than two years after it first became aware of the breach.

185. Section 92 sets out the procedures the competent authority must follow when imposing a penalty. The competent authority is also required to publish a statement of its policy as regards penalties (see sections 93 and 94). Before issuing or altering such a statement, the competent authority must consult on its proposals.

Section 95: Competition scrutiny

186. This section gives the Treasury a power to subject the "regulating provisions" of the competent authority (which is to say the listing rules and general guidance it produces) and its practices to a competition scrutiny regime. The Treasury proposes to use this power to create a competition scrutiny regime for the competent authority which is broadly similar to the regime for the Authority, in its role as financial services regulator, as provided for by Chapter III of Part X of the Act. The power will enable the Treasury to provide for exclusions from the provisions of the Competition Act 1998 analogous to those for which Chapter III of Part X of the Act makes provision.

187. *Subsection (2)* makes clear that such a regime will require the person responsible for the competition scrutiny procedure to consider whether any provision or practice, or combination of provisions and practices, has at any time a significantly adverse effect on competition as defined in *subsections (6) and (7)*.

Section 96: Obligations of issuers of listed securities

188. This section provides that listing rules may place obligations on issuers and may make provision for non-compliance. *Subsection (2)* provides that the competent authority can make listing rules which allow it to publish information which an issuer has been required but has failed to publish.

Section 97: Appointment by competent authority of persons to carry out investigations

189. This section allows the competent authority to appoint investigators if it appears to it that there are circumstances suggesting that there may have been a breach of the listing rules; that a director or former director of an issuer was knowingly concerned in a breach; or that there has been a contravention of the criminal offences in sections 83, 85, or 98. The section applies the provisions of Part XI as if the investigator were appointed under section 167(1). This means that the procedures set out in section 170 must be followed and that the investigator will have the powers set out in section 171.

Section 98: Advertisements etc in connection with listing applications

190. This section makes it an offence to issue an advertisement or other information of a kind specified in listing rules (for example an invitation to purchase securities) unless the contents have been approved by the competent authority or the issue of an unapproved advertisement or information has been authorised by the competent authority. This offence only applies where listing particulars are, or are to be, published.

191. *Subsection (3)* provides a defence against this criminal offence where someone reasonably believed that the advertisement had been approved or its issue authorised by the competent authority.

Section 100: Penalties

192. This section provides that the competent authority must not seek to recover its costs when imposing financial penalties. It also provides that it must operate a scheme to redistribute monies received from financial penalties to issuers. It must consult on the scheme and have regard to representations before making the scheme. The provisions of this section are analogous to those applying to the Authority more generally under paragraph 16 of Schedule 1.

Section 102: Exemption from liability in damages

193. This section gives the competent authority and its staff immunity against legal action for damages in respect of anything done or omitted in the discharge of its functions. This immunity does not apply where the act or omission was in bad faith or where it was unlawful as a result of section 6(1) of the Human Rights Act 1998. Section 6(1) of that Act makes it unlawful for a public authority to act in a way which is incompatible with a right conferred by the European Convention on Human Rights and Fundamental Freedoms which is included in Schedule 1 to the 1998 Act.

Part Vii: Control of Business Transfers

194. This Part provides a mechanism for transferring, with the sanction of the courts, all or part of the business of certain kinds of authorised persons. In broad terms, the mechanism covers 2 types of transfer:

- transfers of insurance business; and
- transfers of banking business.

195. The mechanism, as it relates to transfers of insurance business, replaces the arrangements under sections 49 to 52B of, and Schedule 2C to, the Insurance Companies Act 1982, which implement requirements of the EC insurance directives. Banking business transfers have usually required a private act of Parliament, which can involve a lenghty procedure and substantial cost to the firms concerned.

Section 104: Control of business transfers

196. This section establishes that the arrangements under Part VII are generally the exclusive route for giving effect to the types of transfer to which the Part applies. However, the definition of insurance business transfer schemes under section 105 provides for qualifying cross-border transfers to be approved in other member States, in accordance with the directives.

Section 105: Insurance business transfer schemes

197. This section defines the insurance business transfers covered by the new mechanism. It only applies to transfer schemes where, after the transfer, the business transferred will be carried on from an establishment in the EEA, and where prior to the transfer all or part of the business to be transferred is:

- carried on, wholly or in part, in the EEA by a "UK authorised person" (defined in *subsection (8)*); or
- reinsurance business and it is carried on in the UK branch of an EEA firm (see Schedule 3); or
- carried on, wholly or in part, in the United Kingdom by an authorised person who is neither a UK authorised person nor an EEA firm.

198. In each case the authorised person transferring the business must have the appropriate permission under Part IV of, or Schedule 3 to, the Act.

199. However, *subsection (3)* sets out a series of cases for which the new mechanism does not apply. The mechanism does not apply where the transferor is a friendly society (referred to as case 1). Such transfers are covered by provisions in the Friendly Societies Act 1992. The other cases are where the arrangements under this Part do not apply are:

- transfers of reinsurance business by UK authorised persons which have been approved by a court in another EEA State or by the relevant regulator in the State or States in which it is carried on (case 2);
- transfers of business carried on outside the EEA which do not include policies (other than reinsurance policies) against risks arising in the EEA, and which have been approved by the courts or relevant authorities in a non-EEA State (case 3);
- where each of the policyholders has consented to the transfer, in cases of reinsurance business and entities where the policyholders are 'controllers' (within the meaning of Part XII) of the firm or other firms in the same group, essentially "captive" insurers (case 4).

200. *Subsections (5) to (7)* ensure that the powers of a court to make orders under the Companies Act (and the equivalent Northern Ireland provisions) dealing with schemes for reconstruction (compromises or arrangements agreed with creditors) can apply in transfers covered by the arrangements under the Part.

*Section 106: **Banking business transfer schemes***

201. This section enables parties to a transfer of business involving accepting deposits to apply to the court for an order sanctioning the transfer. *Subsection (1)* applies the arrangements under this part to transfers of the business of authorised persons domiciled in the United Kingdom with permission to accept deposits, wherever the business is carried on. It also applies the arrangements where an overseas firm carrying on banking business in the United Kingdom transfers its business to another firm. However, the arrangements do not apply to transfers from building societies (for which separate arrangements exist under the Building Societies Act 1986) or credit unions or transfers falling within section 427A of the Companies Act.

*Section 107: **Application for order sanctioning transfer scheme***

202. This section enables either a transferee, or the transferor, or both, to apply to the court for an order sanctioning a transfer of an insurance or banking business. *Subsection (3)* makes provision as to the court to which an application may be made. The appropriate court will depend on the country or territory in which the businesses are registered or have their head office.

*Section 108: **Requirements on applicants***

203. This section confers on the Treasury a power to specify, by regulations, requirements with which firms must comply before seeking an order sanctioning a transfer under section 111. Where firms have not complied with those requirements, the court would not be able to sanction the transfer.

204. *Subsection (3)* confirms that regulations made under this section may include requirements to give notice and the way in which notice must be given. This may, for example, include giving notice of the proposed transfer to customers or creditors of the firm but the kinds of requirement are not limited.

205. Regulations made under this power may also specify the circumstances in which the court may decide that a firm need not comply with a requirement. This is necessary to ensure that in circumstances where a firm cannot reasonably comply with a requirement, it need not prevent a court from approving a transfer. An example where this might be necessary is in relation to a requirement to give notice to customers of the firm transferring its business to another, in circumstances where it did not have contact details for some of its customers, as sometimes happens in the case of dormant bank accounts or old life insurance policies.

Section 109: Scheme reports

206. Under this section, it is a requirement that a proposal to transfer insurance business is to be accompanied by a report by an expert. The coverage of the report may be determined by the Authority and the appointment of the expert is subject to the approval of the Authority. The purpose of this section is to ensure that the court is presented with a full and accurate report of the proposed transfer by an independent expert in order that the court may properly assess its impact, including the effect on policyholders of the authorised person in question (and any third parties who may rely on their policies).

Section 110: Right to participate in proceedings

207. This section gives the Authority and those affected by the proposed transfer a right to be heard by the court when it is considering an application under section 107. This will mean that the Authority will be able to make representations about matters which, as regulator, cause it concern. It also ensures that any person connected with either the transferor or transferee firm - including customers of either firm or their employees - may also make representations to the court about the implications for them. The court will be able to take these views into account when considering the application.

Section 107: Sanction of the court for business transfer schemes

208. This section sets out the conditions that must be met before the court may sanction a business transfer scheme. The conditions are that the transferee firm has obtained any necessary certificates, which are set out in Schedule 12, and also that court is satisfied that the firm will have the necessary authorisation to carry on that business after the transfer (unless no authorisation is required, as may be the case for some reinsurance undertakings in other territories).

209. The precise requirements imposed under the Schedule will depend on a number of factors including whether the business in question is insurance or banking business, and the location of the business (that is whether it is domiciled in the United Kingdom, another EEA member State or overseas).

210. An insurance business will require:

- a certificate about confirming that it has the necessary margin of solvency (paragraph 2 of the Schedule); and
- a certificate indicating that a host State regulator - in cases involving risks or firms located in another EEA member State - has consented (or failed to object within 3 months) to the transfer (paragraphs 3 to 5).

211. In the case of a bank it will need to produce:

- a certificate confirming that the bank has adequate resources; and

- in the case where either the transferor or transferee company is domiciled in another EEA state, a certificate confirming that the home state regulator has been informed about the transfer.

212. In deciding whether to sanction the scheme, the court must consider whether it is appropriate, in all the circumstances, to do so.

Section 112: Effect of order sanctioning business transfer scheme

213. This section makes it clear that any order of the court sanctioning a business transfer scheme may include any necessary provisions to ensure that any transfer is able to take proper effect. Accordingly, the court will be able to order either that all rights and liabilities of and against the firm whose business is being transferred become rights and liabilities of the transferee firm, or that appropriate measures are taken to extinguish or reduce such rights and liabilities.

214. A reduction may be necessary, for example, where a firm is insolvent and the transfer of business is part of a "rescue" proposal. In other cases, rights and liabilities may not be suitable for transfer and so alternative arrangements may be required, for example in the case where a bank had a taken a floating charge over the assets of the firm in relation to a credit facility, where neither would be relevant to the ongoing business after the transfer.

215. These arrangements are consistent with the previous arrangements under Schedule 2C to the ICA 1982 and relevant companies and insolvency legislation.

Section 113: Appointment of actuary in relation to reduction of benefits

216. This section enables a court, in response to an application from the Authority, to appoint an independent actuary to report on a business transfer in particular circumstances. This is aimed particularly at situations where a company from which business is to be transferred is in financial difficulties and unlikely to be able to meet all of its obligations to policyholders or other creditors. By the application of insolvency law, the policyholders would only be entitled to recover a proportion of the amounts due to them.

217. Section 112 enables the court to sanction a transfer that has the effect of reducing liabilities to policyholders, since in many cases allowing the transfer to a solvent company will be preferable to leaving the policyholder to recover money due from the insolvent insurer. In practice, a transfer would most likely only be approved where the effect was no worse than if it did not go ahead. The purpose of this section is to enable the court to take an informed view about the proposed reduction in benefits, to ensure that policyholders interests are properly protected. A policyholder who suffered loss in such circumstances might be able to make a claim to the compensation scheme under Part XV of the Act.

Section 114: Rights of certain policyholders

218. This section provides that any EEA policyholders whose local law confers on them a right to cancel the policy in the event of a transfer have an adequate opportunity to exercise that right.

Section 115: Certificate for the purpose of insurance business transfers overseas

219. This section is a paving provision for Part III of Schedule 12 which enables the Authority to issue a certificate about the solvency of a UK authorised firm to which insurance business is to be transferred from overseas. Such a certificate would enable the Authority to confirm to a regulatory authority in another EEA member State or Switzerland that the transferee firm was financially sound and able to accept the business being transferred to it.

*Section 116: **Effect of insurance business transfers authorised in other EEA States***

220. This section ensures that, where an insurance business transfer has been approved in another EEA member State in accordance with its domestic procedures, the transfer has effect in UK law. This means that where a person in the United Kingdom has an insurance policy with an EEA company whose business is in another member State, their contract is transferred so that the policyholder continues to enjoy the same rights and to be subject to the same obligations against the new company as they did against the company that issued the original policy.

*Section 117: **Power to modify this Part***

221. This section allows the Treasury by regulations to modify the arrangements in relation to prescribed categories of transfer (for example, to ensure sufficient flexibility to allow for possible exclusions where transfers were subject to approval procedures in overseas jurisdictions). This section also allows the Treasury by regulations to amend the provisions of this Part to provide for its more effective operation.

Part Viii: Penalties for Market Abuse

222. This Part confers power on the Authority to impose penalties for market abuse or to publish a public statement that someone has engaged in market abuse. The Act sets out the kinds of behaviour which will constitute market abuse and places a duty on the Authority to produce a code which will help to determine whether particular behaviour amounts to market abuse. This code will carry evidential weight, and in certain circumstances will provide a defence, or "safe harbour", against allegations of abuse. This Part also gives the Treasury the power to prescribe the coverage of the regime by specifying both the markets and the investments traded on those markets to which it applies. It sets out the procedures the Authority must follow when proposing to impose a penalty. It also confers a right to refer a decision to impose a penalty to the Tribunal.

*Section 118: **Market abuse***

223. This section sets out the behaviour which constitutes market abuse. It also confers on the Treasury an order-making power to specify which markets and which investments come within the scope of this section.

224. *Subsections (1) and (2)* set out the conditions which must be satisfied before behaviour can be regarded as market abuse (and a penalty possibly imposed or statement published). In order to be abuse the behaviour must:

- take place in relation to qualifying investments traded on a market to which the section applies;
- be behaviour of a particular kind, as set out in subsection (2); and
- be behaviour which is likely to be regarded by a regular user of the market as a failure on the part of the person (A) engaged in the behaviour to observe the standards which the regular user would reasonably expect of a person in A's position. The regular user of the market is defined in *subsection (10)* to be a reasonable person who regularly deals on the market. He is intended to represent the distillation of the standards expected by those who regularly use the market.

225. There are three kinds of behaviour set out in subsection (2). Broadly speaking, these are that the behaviour is based on information not generally available to the rest of the market; that the behaviour is likely to give the regular market user a false or misleading impression; or that the regular user would be likely to regard the behaviour as behaviour which would distort the market.

226. *Subsection (6)(a)* brings behaviour which takes place in relation to the subject matter of investments within the definition of behaviour which can be caught by these provisions. This means that, for example, behaviour in relation to a precious metal which affects the price of a futures contract in the metal can potentially be caught by these provisions if it is behaviour which falls within all of the tests set out above. *Subsection (6)(b)* also brings investments within the regime which are not themselves qualifying investments for the purposes of this section, but which are derivatives of a qualifying investment (for example options on options); or whose price or value is expressed by reference to the price or value of qualifying investments, for example spread bets. *Subsection (8)* allows the Authority to provide that behaviour conforming with a particular rule or rules does not amount to market abuse.

*Section 119: **The code***

227. This section places a duty on the Authority to prepare and issue a code which will allow it to set out the kinds of behaviour which, in its opinion, amount or do not amount to market abuse. The purpose of this code is to give guidance as to whether or not behaviour is abusive.

228. *Subsection (2)* makes clear that the code may describe behaviour which, in the opinion of the Authority, either does or does not amount to abuse. (Section 122 provides that a statement in the code that a particular type of behaviour is not an abuse is conclusive evidence of this fact.) It may also set out factors which, in the Authority's opinion, should be taken into account when determining whether an abuse has occurred. An example of such factors might be an individual's expertise or the fact that someone holds a position of particular responsibility. *Subsections (6) to (8)* place the Authority under a duty to publish the code (including any amended or replacement version under *subsections (4) and (5)*). The Authority must consult on its proposed code, or on proposed alterations or replacements under section 121.

*Section 120: **Provisions included in the Authority's code by reference to the City Code***

229. This section enables the Authority to include in the code produced by it under section 119 "safe-harbours" from proceedings for market abuse for behaviour in conformity with the City Code on Takeovers and Mergers produced by the Panel on Takeovers and Mergers. If the Authority includes any such provisions, then behaviour which complies with those provisions does not amount to market abuse (as a result of section 122(1). The approval of the Treasury is required under *subsection (2)* before it can do so.

230. In considering whether market abuse has taken place, *subsection (3)* requires the Authority to keep itself informed as to the way in which the Panel interprets and administers the relevant provisions of the City Code.

*Section 122: **Effect of the code***

231. *Subsection (1)* provides a safe harbour, by making it clear that if a person undertakes any behaviour which the code currently in force specifically states does not amount to market abuse, then he cannot be taken for the purposes of the Act to have abused the market. *Subsection (2)* makes clear that in other circumstances the code may be relied upon insofar as it indicates that the behaviour in question does or does not amount to market abuse.

*Section 123: **Power to impose penalties in cases of market abuse***

232. This section allows the Authority to impose a monetary penalty on any person, whether an authorised person or not, who has engaged in market abuse or has required or encouraged another to engage in market abuse. *Subsection (3)* allows the Authority, as an alternative to imposing a penalty, to publish a public statement that a person

has engaged in market abuse or has required or encouraged another person to do so. *Subsection (2)* provides that the Authority cannot impose a penalty or make a statement where a person has reasonable grounds for believing his behaviour did not constitute market abuse or that he was not requiring or encouraging another to engage in market abuse, or where the person concerned took all reasonable precautions and exercised all due diligence to avoid doing such things. The procedures for taking action under this section are set out in sections 126 and 127.

*Section 124: **Statement of policy***

233. This section places a duty on the Authority to prepare and publish a statement of its policy in respect of penalties under section 123. The Authority will be able to set out in this document the circumstances in which it might impose a penalty and factors it will take into account in deciding what level of penalty to impose.

234. *Subsection (2)* requires that the Authority's policy for determining the amount of a penalty must take into account the effect and seriousness of the behaviour, whether or not it was deliberate or reckless and whether the person who engaged in the abuse was an individual. The Authority may also take into account other matters it considers appropriate. The Authority must consult on the initial version of the statement and on any subsequent changes as provided for in section 125. *Subsection (3)* requires the Authority to include in the statement an indication of when the Authority is to expected to regard a person as benefiting from section 123(2). *Subsection (6)* makes clear that the Authority must then have regard to a statement issued under this section when using its powers.

*Section 128: **Suspension of investigations***

235. This section allows the Authority to direct a recognised investment exchange or recognised clearing house not to conduct an inquiry or to stop any inquiry it is already undertaking where the Authority is, or is considering, carrying out an investigation itself, or imposing a penalty on a person for market abuse.

*Section 129: **Power of court to impose penalty in cases of market abuse***

236. This section allows the Authority to apply to the court to impose a penalty for market abuse where the court is considering whether to grant an injunction under section 381 or order restitution under section 383 in a case of market abuse.

*Section 130: **Guidance***

237. This section allows the Treasury, with the approval of the Attorney General and the Secretary of State, if the need arises, to issue guidance to the relevant prosecuting authorities (as set out in *subsection (3)*). The purpose of this guidance would be to help those authorities in deciding whether a case should be subject to criminal prosecution, or the imposition of penalties under the market abuse provisions, in the area of overlap between these provisions and the criminal offences of insider dealing (in the Criminal Justice Act 1993) and misleading statements and practices (in section 397). *Subsection (5)* confers a power on the Lord Advocate to issue equivalent guidance in relation to Scotland, where there are different arrangements for prosecution of offences.

Part Ix: Hearings and Appeals

238. This Part establishes the Financial Services and Markets Tribunal. Various sections in the Act provide a right to refer a matter to the Tribunal once the Authority has notified the person concerned of its decision. This Part sets out the procedural framework for referrals to the Tribunal and for appeals from the Tribunal to the Court of Appeal, or in Scotland to the Court of Session, on a point of law. The Part gives the Lord Chancellor a general power to make rules for the Tribunal's operation. Schedule 13 sets out further details of the Tribunal's constitution and operation.

239. This Part also confers on the Lord Chancellor a power to establish a scheme to provide subsidised legal assistance in proceedings before the Tribunal for individuals on whom the Authority seeks to impose a penalty for market abuse under Part VIII of the Act.

Section 132: ***The Financial Services and Markets Tribunal***

240. This section establishes the Tribunal and gives the Lord Chancellor the power to set its procedural rules. The Council on Tribunals is given oversight of the new Tribunal under the Tribunal & Inquiries Act 1992. Schedule 13 sets out requirements for the appointment of the President of the Tribunal, and the "panel of chairmen" panel and lay panel from which members of the Tribunal will be drawn. It includes provision for their qualifications and terms of office. It also permits the appointment of a Deputy President and administrative staff. It further provides power for the Tribunal to summon witnesses and to award costs. *Subsection (3)* contains the power for the Lord Chancellor to make rules for the Tribunal. Paragraph 9 of Schedule 13 sets out examples of the aspects of the Tribunal's procedures which might be covered by the Lord Chancellor's rules (such as when hearings might be held in private). *Subsection (4)* provides that this does not limit the Lord Chancellor's power.

Section 133: ***Proceedings: general provision***

241. This section sets the time limit for making a reference to the Tribunal. The time limit is 28 days from the date of the decision notice or supervisory notice, unless a different period is prescribed in the procedural rules made for the Tribunal by the Lord Chancellor under section 132. The Tribunal will also have discretion to allow references to be made after the time limit has expired, subject again to any provision in the Tribunal's procedural rules.

242. The section also makes clear that the Tribunal may hear any evidence it considers relevant in determining the case before it, including evidence that was not available to the Authority when it made its decision. The Tribunal must determine what action the Authority should take and may give directions to the Authority in order to give effect to its determination. The Tribunal may also make recommendations as to the Authority's rules and procedures.

243. A supervisory notice takes effect on the date it specifies. However, *subsection (9)* provides that the Authority may not take the action referred to in a decision notice until the time for making a reference to the Tribunal has expired or, if the case is referred, until the case has been finally disposed of, including any subsequent appeals to the Court of Appeal, Court of Session or House of Lords (see section 137 below). An order of the Tribunal may be enforced as if it were an order of a county court in England, Wales or Northern Ireland, or the Court of Session in Scotland.

Section 134: ***Legal assistance scheme***

244. This section gives the Lord Chancellor the power to make regulations establishing a legal assistance scheme. It sets out the coverage that such a scheme should have, namely that a person should only be eligible for legal assistance if he is an individual who has referred a decision of the Authority to impose on him a penalty for market abuse and provided that he meets the eligibility criteria which are to be established under section 135(1)(d).

Section 135: ***Provisions of the legal assistance scheme***

245. This section gives examples of the type of provision the Lord Chancellor may include in the regulations, for example:

- the form legal assistance may take;
- the persons who may be engaged to provide the assistance;

- eligibility criteria; and
- procedural details as to how an application is made, to whom, and as to what happens when assistance is granted.

*Section 136: **Funding of the legal assistance scheme***

246. This section sets out the way in which the legal assistance scheme is to be funded. It will be a free-standing scheme rather than an extension of legal aid and will be paid for by levies raised from authorised persons. The Lord Chancellor will determine the potential or actual cost of the legal assistance scheme. The Authority will have responsibility for determining the distribution of levies across the regulated community, collecting them and paying them over to the Lord Chancellor's Department.

247. The money raised will be paid into the Consolidated Fund. Spending on the legal assistance scheme will be voted expenditure. The costs of administering the scheme will come out of the running costs of the Tribunal.

248. If the amount paid to the Lord Chancellor in any one year exceeds the cost of the legal assistance scheme (for example because the costs in that period prove to be lower than anticipated), he must decide either to repay the excess to the Authority or else take into account this amount in the next determination of costs, by reducing the amount which the Authority has to levy during the following year. If the excess amount is repaid to the Authority, the Authority has discretion whether to distribute the money amongst those persons upon whom the levy was imposed (or some of them) to offset it against future invoices, or else partly to distribute the amount and partly offset it. This enables the Authority to avoid costly redistribution of small amounts. If the Authority considers that it is not practicable to deal with an excess in any of these ways, it may obtain the permission of the Lord Chancellor to use it in some other appropriate manner.

*Section 137: **Appeal on a point of law***

249. This section establishes the right to appeal to the Court of Appeal or Court of Session on a point of law against a decision of the Tribunal. An appeal may be brought only with the permission of the Tribunal or the appeal court. If the appeal court considers that the decision is wrong in law it may remit the matter back to the Tribunal for a rehearing and decision or make a decision itself. An appeal may be made from the Court of Appeal or Court of Session to the House of Lords with the leave of the Court or the House of Lords. The Lord Chancellor may make procedural rules in relation to the exercise of these appeal rights.

Part X: Rules and Guidance

250. This Part of the Act confers powers upon the Authority and the Treasury to set regulatory requirements for authorised persons. It also gives the Authority power to issue guidance on requirements imposed by or under the Act.

Chapter I: Rule-Making Powers

251. Chapter I concerns the Authority's basic rule-making powers, the purpose for which rules can be made and the scope of the powers. There are other rule-making powers for specific purposes in relevant parts of the Act, including Parts XV, XVI, XVII, XX and XXII. This Chapter also sets out the relevant procedural requirements when making rules.

252. Parts V, VIII, XIX, and XX also contain specific powers which enable the Authority to impose requirements on particular classes of person. For example, through statements of principle, codes of practice and directions on approved persons; on any person in relation to market abuse; on members of Lloyd's; and on members of the

professions. Those powers are described in the relevant Parts of these explanatory notes.

Section 138: General rule-making power

253. This section confers a power on the Authority to make rules applying to authorised persons with respect to their carrying on of regulated and unregulated activities. Rules made under this section are referred to as "general rules" and can only be made to protect the interests of consumers. There need not be a direct relationship between the authorised persons to whom the rules apply and the consumers who are protected by the rules - so, for example, the Authority will be able to make rules under this section to protect the interests of beneficiaries of trusts, to further market integrity, as required by the Investment Services Directive, or to protect against systemic risk.

254. The bulk of the Authority's handbook of rules and guidance will be constructed using the rule-making power in this section. The power will also enable the Authority to make other rules, including rules relating to firms' systems and controls and rules regulating the conduct of firms' business with customers. These could, for example, include "know your customer" rules and "disclosure" requirements.

255. The provisions in this section enable the Authority to make rules at differing levels of detail, from rules with a high level of generality, which the Authority refers to as principles, to detailed conduct of business provisions.

256. Sections 152 to 155 set down the procedural requirements which the Authority must follow when making rules.

Section 139: Miscellaneous ancillary matters

257. This section elaborates on the provisions which the Authority can make under the rule-making powers. It expressly enables the Authority to make rules in respect of the handling of client money by authorised persons. The rules could be used to require money to be held in trust.

258. This section also allows the Authority to make rules which require authorised persons to allow customers a "cooling off" period after entering into an agreement. For example, under section 76 of the ICA 1982, persons entering long-term insurance contracts have 14 days in which to cancel the policy and recover any premium paid. This section would allow the Authority to make rules requiring authorised persons to extend similar rights to customers.

Section 141: Insurance business rules

259. This section empowers the Authority to make insurance business rules prohibiting an authorised person who has permission to deal in contracts of insurance from carrying on a specified activity, which may be a non-regulated activity.

260. *Subsection (3)* enables the Authority to make rules in relation to contracts of long-term insurance entered into by an authorised person in the course of carrying on his business, in particular restricting the descriptions of property, or indices of value, by reference to which the benefits under such contracts may be determined.

Section 142: Insurance business: regulations supplementing Authority's rules

261. This section enables the Treasury to make regulations applicable to non-authorised persons connected with authorised persons with permission in relation to contracts of insurance, preventing them from taking actions which would weaken the effect of "asset identification rules" made by the Authority under the powers in this Part. Breaches of these regulations are subject to criminal sanctions.

262. *Subsection (3)* gives the Treasury powers to make regulations which would prevent a company paying dividends or creating a mortgage or charge over its property, and which would make void any mortgages or charges made, in breach of those regulations.

*Section 143: **Endorsement of codes etc***

263. This section confers a power on the Authority to make rules endorsing the City Code on Takeovers and Mergers ("the Takeover Code") and the Substantial Acquisition Rules ("SARs"), or particular provisions of them.

264. This section provides a mechanism enabling the Authority to exercise its disciplinary powers over authorised persons for a breach of the endorsed provisions of the Takeover Code or SARs. The arrangements are designed to ensure that an adviser will cease to act where the Takeover Code or SARs have been breached. *Subsections (3)* and *(4)* have the effect that disciplinary or intervention powers in respect of endorsed provisions may be taken by the Authority if the Takeover Panel has requested it to do so.

265. Before making rules which endorse the Takeover Code or the SARs, the Authority must follow the usual procedures set out in section 155 for consulting on a draft of the proposed rules. By applying relevant provisions of section 155, *subsection (8)* of this section also requires the Authority to consult if it wishes to give a notification to the Takeover Panel that it considers the Panel's own consultation procedures are satisfactory. If the Authority does give such a notification, the effect under *subsections (6) and (7)* is that the Authority's endorsement of the Code or SARs extends automatically to subsequent amendments of the Code or SARs.

*Section 144: **Price stabilising rules***

266. This section allows the Authority to make rules regarding actions which may be taken by authorised firms to stabilise the price of investments. Section 397(4) and 397(5)(b) provide that a person who is alleged to have created a false or misleading impression as to the market in certain investments has a defence to a charge under that section (such as misleading statements) if he proves that he was acting in conformity with rules made under this section.

267. *Subsection (5)* provides that the Authority may make rules which provide a similar defence to persons who have stabilised investments in compliance with the price stabilisation rules of an overseas body which is specified by the Authority. If an overseas body which is specified under this section changes its rules, the amended body's rules will be taken by the Authority to be endorsed under this section if the Authority has confirmed that it is satisfied with the overseas body's consultation procedures.

268. *Subsection (4)* confers on the Treasury a power to make regulations setting the outer boundaries of the Authority's power to make price stabilising rules.

*Section 145: **Financial promotion rules***

269. This section confers a power on the Authority to make rules applying to authorised persons in relation to the regulation of financial promotion under Parts II and XVII of the Act.

270. *Subsection (3)* enables the Treasury to restrict this power.

*Section 147: **Control of information rules***

271. *Subsection (1)* enables the Authority to make rules about the disclosure and use of information held by an authorised person. These rules are commonly known as "Chinese walls" rules. Chinese walls are barriers in the form of procedures, systems, management and physical separation which firms may employ in order to ensure that information obtained by one part of a firm is not communicated in inappropriate

circumstances to another part of the firm (for example, where it would advantage one client at the expense of another). This power is broadly in line with that currently contained in section 48(2)(h) of the FS Act 1986.

272. Under *subsections (2)(a) and (c)*, rules may require that information be withheld or not used for a customer's benefit where it would otherwise have to be disclosed or used, while *subsections (2)(b) and (d)* provide that rules may specify circumstances in which an authorised person may withhold or not use information which would otherwise have to be disclosed or used. This means that, if an authorised person maintains Chinese walls in accordance with Authority rules made under the section, then he will not be subject to obligations as to the disclosure and use of information that would otherwise apply.

Section 148: ***Modification or waiver of rules***

273. This section concerns the power of the Authority to waive or modify certain kinds of rules, as set out in *subsection (1),* at the request of an authorised person or with their consent. *Subsection (4)* specifies the circumstances in which the Authority may waive or modify these rules.

274. Waivers or modifications of rules can have indefinite effect or can be revoked by the Authority. Breaches of conditions attached to a waiver or modification are equivalent to a breach of rules.

275. *Subsections (6) and (7)* concern the obligation on the Authority to publish rule waivers or modifications. They provide that the Authority must publish waivers or modifications in such a way as to bring them to the attention of the people who are likely to be affected, unless the Authority thinks it would be inappropriate to do so. In considering whether publication would be appropriate, the Authority should take into account whether it believes that publication would unreasonably prejudice the authorised person's commercial interests or contravene any international obligations of the United Kingdom. The Authority would also need to take into account whether a breach of the rule in question would give rise to a right of action by a person under section 150. Persons affected by the modification or waiver will include clients of the authorised person and other authorised persons who might wish to benefit from similar arrangements.

276. In deciding whether certain of the conditions for withholding publication are met, *subsection (8)* requires the Authority to consider whether it can publish a waiver or modification of a rule without disclosing the identity of the authorised person concerned.

Section 149: ***Evidential provisions***

277. This section enables the Authority to make rules which, if breached, will not lead to any disciplinary or other sanction provided for under the Act. Rules made under this section must state that they will not give rise to sanctions under the Act, but they must also indicate that their contravention can be relied on as indicating that another rule has been contravened, or that compliance with the rule can be relied on as indicating that another rule has been complied with. In particular, this power will enable the Authority to elaborate on rules, including principles, which are framed at a higher level of generality. The power can be used to promulgate codes, such as a code of practice, whereby rules comprising the code carry evidential status as to whether a higher level principle, which is underpinned by the code, has been breached.

Section 150: ***Actions for damages***

278. This section sets out the circumstances in which persons who suffer loss as a result of a rule breach by an authorised person have a right of action for damages for resulting losses. This section does not remove any common law cause of action which a person

might otherwise have. It allows a class of people to recover losses just by showing that there has been a breach of a rule as a result of which they have suffered loss rather then having to rely on that breach as evidence of negligence.

279. The section creates a presumption that private persons (as defined by the Treasury) who suffer loss as a result of a rule breach have a right of action for damages. The right does not extend to breaches of financial resources rules, listing rules or other rules which may be specified by the Authority. Customers would only generally suffer loss as a result of a breach of financial resources rules if the authorised person concerned became insolvent. In those circumstances, the relevant person's rights in the insolvency would not be altered by a separate right of action. Additionally, it might not be appropriate to attach a right of action to certain other rules, such as those drawn at a high level of generality.

280. There is a presumption that persons other than private persons do not have a right of action for damages, although the Treasury may by regulations specify that breaches of certain rules are actionable by non-private persons.

*Section 151: **Limits on effect of contravening rules***

281. Breach of the Authority's rules does not make a person guilty of an offence, nor does it make a transaction unenforceable or void.

*Section 152: **Notification of rules to the Treasury***

282. This section places a requirement on the Authority to give copies of new rules to the Treasury or, when it amends or revokes a rule, to give written notice of the fact to the Treasury.

*Section 153: **Rule-making instruments***

283. This section requires the Authority to publish its rules in writing. As a result of *subsection (3)*, if rules do not specify the power under which they are made, they will not have effect.

*Section 155: **Consultation***

284. This section imposes consultation requirements on the Authority when it proposes to exercise its rule-making powers. Generally, draft rules issued for consultation must, as a result of *subsection (2)*, be accompanied by a cost-benefit analysis of the proposals, an explanation of the purpose of the proposed rules and a statement that representations about the Authority's proposals may be made to the Authority within a specified time. They must also be accompanied by a statement of the Authority's reasons for believing that the proposed rules are compatible with its objectives.

285. *Subsection (4)* provides that the Authority must have regard to representations made to it when consulting on proposals to make rules. *Subsections (5) and (6)* provide that if the Authority decides to make the rule, it must give a feedback statement on the representations it received. If the rules which are introduced differ significantly from those which the Authority consulted on, the Authority must publish a statement of that fact, together with a cost-benefit analysis concerning the new provisions.

286. The Authority does not have to prepare a cost-benefit analysis when it considers that its proposals will not result in a material increase in costs. It would, however, still need to consult on the content of the proposed rules. Also, where the Authority proposes to exercise its powers to charge fees, the requirement to produce a cost-benefit analysis does not apply but the Authority is required to consult on the proposed expenditure which would result from the fee-raising exercise. Part III of Schedule 1 contains further provisions regarding the Authority's fee-raising powers.

287. Consultation requirements will not apply if the Authority considers that any delay resulting from the consultation would harm consumers.

Section 156: General supplementary powers

288. This section confirms that the Authority's rules may make different provision for different cases and that the rules may make incidental, supplemental, consequential and transitional provisions.

Chapter II: Guidance

289. Chapter II concerns the Authority's power to issue and charge for guidance on its rules, the legislation and other matters relating to its functions, including its regulatory objectives.

Section 157: Guidance

290. This section enables the Authority to issue and charge for guidance on all the matters listed in *subsection (1)*.

291. *Subsection (2)* confirms that the Authority can use its financial resources or its other resources to support the giving of information and advice by third parties where the Authority considers it could have given the advice or information under this section.

292. *Subsection (3)* provides that when giving guidance on its rules which is intended to have broad application, the Authority will need to meet various of the requirements of section 155, including those requiring consultation and the publication of a cost-benefit analysis. *Subsection (4)* clarifies that the Authority can charge for its guidance, whether it is offered generally or in response to a specific request.

Chapter III: Competition Scrutiny

293. Chapter III provides for competition scrutiny of the Authority's rules, guidance, codes and practices.

Section 160: Reports by the Director General of Fair Trading

294. This section concerns reports by the DGFT on possible adverse effects on competition of the Authority's regulating provisions and practices. A significant adverse effect on competition is defined in section 159(2) and (3). It includes things which have the effect of requiring or encouraging exploitation of the strength of a market position.

295. *Subsection (1)* provides that the DGFT must keep the Authority's practices and regulating provisions (which are defined in section 159 and include rules, guidance and codes) under review. The DGFT can, at any time, investigate the Authority's practices and regulating provisions under the powers conferred by section 161.

296. Following an investigation, if the DGFT finds that regulating provisions or practices, either singly or in combination, have a significant adverse effect on competition then he must produce a report. The DGFT has discretion as to whether to produce a report or not if he finds that there is no such effect.

297. *Subsections (5) and (6)* provide that the DGFT must send a copy of any report he produces to the Competition Commission (the "Commission"), the Treasury and the Authority. The DGFT must, so far as is practicable, exclude from the published version of the report any matter which relates to the affairs of a person which might seriously prejudice that person's interests. (*Subsection (9)* provides that such matters do not need to be excluded from the version which goes to the Commission, the Treasury and the Authority.)

Section 161: Power of Director to request information

298. This section provides that, in carrying out his functions under section 160, the DGFT has powers to request relevant documents from any person, and to request relevant information from any business.

299. *Subsections (5) and (6)* provide that if a person fails to produce a required document, or piece of information, then the DGFT may report the matter to the court, and if the court is satisfied that there was no reasonable excuse for this failure, that person may be dealt with as if he were in contempt of court.

Section 162: Consideration by the Competition Commission

300. This section concerns the role and duties of the Competition Commission following receipt of a report from the DGFT. It is supplemented by the provisions of Schedule 14.

301. There are two types of report which the Commission must consider under this section and on which it must produce a report. The first is a report by the DGFT which concludes that particular regulating provisions or practices of the Authority have a significantly adverse effect on competition (type A). The second is a report by the DGFT which concludes that particular regulating provisions or practices do not have such an effect, but where the DGFT has referred the matter to the Commission for further consideration (type B). (If the DGFT does not ask the Commission to consider a type B report, then that is the end of the matter.)

302. *Subsection (4)* provides that the Commission's report must state its conclusions as to whether the regulatory provisions or practices have a significantly adverse effect on competition. If it concludes that there is no such effect (that is, it agrees with a type B report or disagrees with a type A report), then that is the end of the matter. No further action can be taken.

303. If, however, the Commission concludes that there is such an effect, then *subsection (5)* requires it to state in its report whether it considers that the effect is justified. In taking this decision, *subsection (7)* requires the Commission, as far as is reasonably possible, to reach a conclusion which the Authority could have reached given the obligations which the Act places on the Authority and the functions which it confers. In its report, the Commission has to state what action, if any, ought to be taken by the Authority in the light of the unjustified anti-competitive effect. This could include the Authority changing its rules or practices in specified ways.

304. Any report produced by the Commission under this section has to be sent to the Treasury, the Authority and the DGFT. *Subsection (2)* provides that the Commission does not need to produce a report where there has been a change of circumstances which makes it unnecessary. For example, the Authority may, once it has received the DGFT's report, change the rule in question, or stop engaging in a particular practice, so that the adverse effect on competition identified by the DGFT is removed.

Section 163: Role of the Treasury

305. This section concerns the Treasury's powers to take action following an adverse report from the Commission.

306. If the Commission's report is that the significantly adverse effect on competition is not justified, *subsection (2)* requires the Treasury, unless exceptional circumstances exist, to direct the Authority to take appropriate action. *Subsection (4)* provides that the Treasury must have regard to the Commission's conclusion as expressed in its report. The special circumstances in which the Treasury do not have to direct the Authority to make changes following an adverse Commission report are where:

- the Authority has already taken action, for example through changes to its rules or practices, which means that the Commission's recommendations are no longer relevant; or
- the Treasury concludes that the existence of exceptional circumstances mean that it would not be appropriate or necessary to direct the Authority to make changes. For example, the Treasury may conclude that there would be a grave risk to the financial system if certain regulating provisions were changed.

307. *Subsection (7)* provides that the Authority cannot be directed by the Treasury to take any action which it would not have the power to take itself. If the Commission were to recommend changes which did not, for example, provide an appropriate level of protection for consumers, the Treasury could not direct the Authority to make those changes.

308. If the Commission's view is that a significantly adverse effect is justified, *subsections (5) and (6)* allow the Treasury to override that decision and direct the Authority to make changes where there are exceptional circumstances, for example, in order to meet international obligations.

309. *Subsections (10), (11) and (12)* provide that if the Treasury decide, because of exceptional circumstances, not to take action following a Commission report that a regulating provision or practice has an adverse effect on competition, or decide to take action in the opposite case, they must produce a statement giving their reasons. Any such statement must be made available to the public and must be laid before Parliament.

Section 164: The Competition Act 1998

310. This section makes clear that neither the prohibition in Chapter I (of agreements preventing, restricting or distorting competition within the United Kingdom) nor the prohibition in Chapter II (of abuse of a dominant position in a market which may effect trade in the United Kingdom) of the Competition Act 1998 apply to any action taken by a person in order to comply with the Authority's regulating provisions or practices.

Part Xi: Information Gathering & Investigations

311. This Part sets out the powers of the Authority to require the production of information and documents, to require reports to be compiled, to conduct investigations and to obtain access to premises. Many of these powers are also held concurrently by the Secretary of State in recognition of his wider responsibilities in relation to company law.

312. The powers provided for in this Part are in addition to the specific powers conferred on the Authority by other provisions of the Act to request information from unauthorised persons in particular circumstances, such as in connection with an application for authorisation or recognition. They enable the Authority to require information on an ad hoc basis and therefore supplement the Authority's ability to make rules requiring authorised persons to provide it with information on a routine basis under its general rule-making power (section 138).

313. Under section 177, failure to comply with any requirement imposed using any of the powers in this Part can be certified to the court and dealt with by the court as if the defaulter were in contempt.

314. None of the powers in this Part may be used to require the disclosure of material which is protected by section 413.

Section 165: Authority's power to require information

315. This section gives the Authority a general power to require information or documents which may reasonably be required in connection with the discharge of its functions

under the Act. The information or documents may be required from any person, including a legal person, who is any of the following:

- an authorised person;
- a formerly authorised person;
- a person connected with an authorised person, as defined in *subsection (11)*;
- an operator, trustee or depository of an open-ended investment company;
- a recognised investment exchange;
- a recognised clearing house.

316. Either the Authority can write to the person asking for the production of the information or documents within a reasonable timescale, or it can send an officer to whom it has given written authorisation. The person is required to provide the information or documents without delay, and he may also be required to take any reasonable steps the Authority may specify to verify the information provided.

*Section 166: **Reports by skilled persons***

317. This gives the Authority the power to require an authorised person or a formerly authorised person to commission and provide the Authority with a report into any relevant matter the Authority may specify. This must be a matter about which the Authority could require information under section 165, so the report must reasonably be required in connection with the discharge of the Authority's functions.

318. The power also enables the Authority to require such reports from other persons carrying on a business who are, or were, connected to the authorised or formerly authorised person in the ways specified in *subsection (2)*. Essentially, these are members of the same group of companies, or companies closely linked through a common shareholder, or any partnership of which the authorised or formerly authorised person is or was a member. This is a more limited set of persons than under section 165 and Schedule 13.

319. The person making the report must be nominated by the Authority, or his appointment must be approved by it. The Authority has to be satisfied that he has the relevant skills to report on the matter concerned. In many cases this person may be an accountant, or they may be a person with some other suitable professional qualification, such as a lawyer or an actuary, or they may be a person with particular commercial or professional experience, such as a banker. The Authority may also specify the form of the report.

320. *Subsection (5)* imposes an obligation on any in-house expert working for the authorised or connected person to co-operate with the person appointed to produce the report. Thus, if the report is to be produced by an actuary then the in-house actuary who works for the firm is obliged to co-operate in the production of the report. This duty is enforceable by the Authority through an injunction, or a comparable order in Scotland.

*Section 167: **Appointment of persons to carry out general investigations***

321. Under this section, either the Authority or the Secretary of State (the "investigating authority") may, where it appears that there are good reasons for doing so, appoint competent persons to conduct an investigation on their behalf into the business of an authorised person or appointed representative, or into the ownership or control of an authorised person. An "appointed representative" is a person who is exempt from the general prohibition in relation to particular regulated activities by virtue of a contract with an authorised person as described under section 39. An appointed representative and the authorised person who is the principal of that representative as a result of the contract may be investigated at the same time. An investigation may also be made into a formerly authorised person or a former appointed representative, although the

scope of such investigations is limited by *subsection (4)* to the business they conducted while they were authorised or appointed or under the control or ownership of the former authorised person at that time. Written notice must be given to the person under investigation under section 170(2).

322. The people appointed to conduct the investigation may be employees of the investigating authority (under section 170(5)), or other people engaged specifically for the purpose. If they judge it necessary for the purposes of the investigation, they may also inquire into the business of other connected companies or partnerships, including those which were connected at some relevant time in the past (this extends to the same classes of connected company or partnership as section 166). The investigator(s) must give written notice to any other company or partnership whose business they intend to inquire into in this way.

Section 168: ***Appointment of persons to carry out investigations in particular cases***

323. In addition to the general power under section 167 to investigate the business of authorised persons and appointed representatives where there is "good reason" to do so, this section gives the Authority or the Secretary of State ("the investigating authority") the power to appoint competent persons (who can be employees of the investigating authority) to conduct investigations where it appears that there are circumstances suggesting that some specific contravention or offence may have taken place. The more specific grounds for the exercise of the powers under this section are reflected in the wider powers of the investigators (see notes on sections 171 to 173 below).

324. Among the contraventions that may be investigated by either the Authority or the Secretary of State under this section are a breach by an unauthorised person of the general prohibition, the commission of the misleading statements and practices offence under section 397, market abuse under section 118, or insider dealing under Part V of the Criminal Justice Act 1993. The Authority, but not the Secretary of State, may also launch an investigation under this section where a person is suspected of having committed an offence under prescribed money laundering regulations.

325. The Authority may also appoint investigators under this section to look into suspected contraventions of rules or regulations made under the Act, failures to comply with statements of principle made under section 64, or to investigate the fitness and properness of approved persons under Part V of the Act. The fitness and properness of authorised persons may be investigated under section 167.

Section 169: ***Investigations etc in support of overseas regulator***

326. This section gives the Authority new powers comparable to those held concurrently by the Treasury and the Secretary of State under section 82 of the Companies Act 1989 to investigate matters on behalf of an overseas regulator. In deciding whether it is appropriate to exercise this power to require information or to appoint investigators on behalf of an overseas authority, the Authority is directed to take account of the factors listed in *subsection (4)*, which include the seriousness of the case and the wider public interest in providing the assistance.

327. When the request comes from another competent authority under any of the single market directives (see the notes on Schedule 3 for a brief explanation), the Authority is also required to consider whether the assistance must be given in order to fulfil the obligations to co-operate imposed by those directives. If it decides that it is, the other factors fall away.

328. The Authority may make the exercise of the power conditional on the overseas authority making an appropriate contribution towards the cost of doing so, except where it considers that exercise is necessary in order to fulfil the obligations to co-operate under the directives.

329. Under *subsection (7)*, the Authority may decide to permit representatives to attend and participate in any interview to be conducted by the investigators it has appointed. But in order to permit this, the Authority is required to be satisfied that the information thus obtained by the overseas regulator will be subject to equivalent safeguards on its subsequent use and disclosure as are contained in Part XXIII of the Act. The Authority must also prepare a statement of its policy on the exercise of this discretion, which must be approved by the Treasury and, if approved, published. The discretion may not be exercised until this statement has been approved and published.

*Section 170: **Investigations: general***

330. Where an investigation has been launched into a person under section 167 or 168, the Authority or the Secretary of State (whichever is the investigating authority) must notify that person that the investigator has been appointed.. They must also inform the person under investigation of the reason for the appointment, and the particular provisions of the Act under which the appointment has been made.

331. However no notification is needed for investigations under section 168 into possible insider dealing, market abuse or misleading statements and practices, or into contraventions of the general prohibition under section 19, the financial promotion prohibition under section 21 or the prohibition on promoting collective investment schemes under section 238, since in those cases the investigator may not know the identity of the perpetrator or may be looking into market circumstances at the outset of the investigation rather than investigating a particular person. Nor is notification required if the investigating authority believes that it would be likely to result in the investigation being frustrated.

332. *Subsection (5)* allows employees of the investigating authority to act as investigators under this Part of the Act.

333. *Subsections (7) and (8)* allow the investigating authority to control the scope, timetable and form of the investigation by issuing directions to the investigator(s). Any directions must be notified to the person under investigation under *subsection (9)* except for those types of investigation where initial notice is not required, or where the investigating authority believes that notification would be likely to result in the investigation being frustrated.

*Section 171: **Powers of persons appointed under** section 167*

334. This section establishes the powers of investigators appointed under the general investigations power to require people to attend before them and answer questions, and to provide information or documents. The investigators may only impose these requirements where they reasonably consider that the questions, information or documents in question are relevant to the investigation. And they may only impose them on the person under investigation, or any other "connected person" as defined in *subsection (4)*. These limitations reflect the broad grounds on which the general investigatory power is exercisable.

*Section 172: **Additional power of persons appointed under** section 168(1) **or (4)***

335. This section establishes wider powers for investigators appointed under section 168(1) or (4), the power to investigate particular suspected contraventions or offences. It does not, therefore, apply to investigations into possible insider dealing, market abuse, misleading statements and practices or a breach of the general prohibition or the promotional prohibitions. Because the grounds required under section 168 are more specific, the powers available to the investigator are wider in terms of who may be required to give information. A person who is not the person under investigation or connected to that person may only be asked questions so long as the investigator is satisfied that it is necessary or expedient to do so. The term "connected" attracts the same meaning as under section 171.

Section 173: Powers of persons appointed as a result of section 168(2)

336. This section establishes wider powers for investigators appointed to investigate possible insider dealing, market abuse, misleading statements and practices or a breach of the general or the promotional prohibitions under sections 19, 21 or 238. Because these are liable to focus, at least initially, on market circumstances rather than the conduct or circumstances of any particular person, or the activities of persons unknown, there is no requirement to notify a particular person as the subject of the investigation. So the concept of connectedness does not apply. The investigator can require any person to attend and answer questions, or to supply information or documents, so long as the investigator considers that they may be able to give information relevant to the investigation.

Section 174: Admissibility of statements made to investigators

337. A statement made by a person in compliance with a requirement imposed by an investigator under this Part is generally admissible in any proceedings. But it may not be adduced against the person who made the statement, or questions relating to it asked, by the prosecution in criminal proceedings other than for the charges listed in *subsection (3)*, nor by the Authority in proceedings before the Tribunal to determine whether a penalty should be imposed for, or a public statement made in respect of, market abuse. It may, however, be adduced, or a question relating to it may be asked, by the person himself, or by those acting on his behalf. It can be used by the prosecution or the Authority in cases against another person, or in cases against that person where the charge is one of those listed in *subsection (3)*. All of the charges mentioned in that subsection relate to the provision of false information.

338. The section is necessary to take into account the judgment by the European Court of Human Rights in the Saunders case ((1997) 23 E.H.H.R. 313).

Section 175: Information and documents: supplemental provisions

339. This section enables the Authority or an investigator appointed by either the Authority or the Secretary of State under this Part to compel the production of a document by a person who is holding a document on behalf of another person if they would have the power to compel the latter to produce the document if they held it. If any person required to produce a document fails to do so, they may be compelled to state where, to the best of their knowledge, the document is.

340. A document once obtained may be copied or have extracts taken from it, and the person producing the document, or any other relevant person, may be required to explain it. But the production of a document does not affect any rights a third party may have over it.

341. Documents subject to banking confidentiality may also be withheld unless the person holding the information, or the person to whom the duty of confidence is owed, is the person under investigation or a related company, or the person to whom the duty is owed consents to its disclosure, or the requirement to disclose has been specifically authorised by the Authority or the Secretary of State.

Section 176: Entry of premises under warrant

342. An investigator appointed by the Authority or the Secretary of State may obtain a warrant for entry to any premises from a justice of the peace, or in Scotland from a justice of the peace or a sheriff. Such a warrant can then be executed by a police constable (*subsection (5)* sets out what the constable may do in the exercise of the warrant).

343. To issue the warrant the justice of the peace or sheriff must be satisfied that there are reasonable grounds for believing:

- a request for information under this Part has not been wholly complied with, and that the documents or information may be found on the premises concerned; or
- the premises are the business premises of an authorised person or appointed representative, that information or documents on those premises could be required by the Authority or the investigator, but that a request for that information or those documents would not be complied with, or would result in the information or documents being removed, tampered with or destroyed; or
- a serious offence has or is in the process of being committed, and that there is information or are documents on those premises which are relevant to that offence, which could be required by the Authority or the investigator, but which would not be produced, or which might be removed, tampered with or destroyed.

344. *Subsections (6) and (7)* apply to these warrants certain safeguards and other protections that apply to warrants issued under the Police and Criminal Evidence Act 1984 and the equivalent order in Northern Ireland. This includes giving the constable the right to employ reasonable force to gain entry.

345. *Subsection (8)* provides for documents seized under a warrant to be held for up to 3 months, or for longer if relevant proceedings are instituted during that period.

*Section 177: **Offences***

346. If a person fails to comply with a requirement imposed under this Part without a reasonable excuse, the Authority or the Secretary of State may certify the fact to a court and the court may then deal with the person as if he were in contempt. A person who intentionally obstructs the exercise of any rights conferred by a warrant under the preceding section is guilty of a criminal offence and liable on summary conviction to a prison term of up to 3 months, or a fine up to level 5 on the standard scale (£5,000), or both.

347. A person who knowingly or recklessly provides false or misleading information in response to a requirement under this Part also commits an offence. On summary conviction he would be liable to a prison term of up to 6 months, or a fine up to the statutory maximum (£5,000), or both. On indictment he would be liable to a prison term of up to 2 years, or a fine, or both.

348. The same penalties would be available against anyone who knows or suspects that an investigation is likely to be conducted and falsifies, conceals, destroys or disposes of any document he knows or suspects to be relevant, or causes such a document to be falsified, concealed, destroyed or disposed of.

Part Xii: Control Over Authorised Persons

349. This Part is concerned with persons who intend to acquire control over UK authorised persons by virtue of their shareholding or voting rights. The Part also deals with increases and decreases in the extent of a person's control. Specifically, a person who proposes either to acquire control or to increase the level of their control must notify the Authority and secure its approval. The Authority may object to a particular acquisition or increase in control or it may attach certain conditions to its approval. A person proposing to decrease their control must merely notify the Authority of their intention. A breach of the obligations imposed by this Part is a criminal offence. The requirements in this Part are necessary to meet certain single market directive obligations. They carry forward similar requirements in the predecessor legislation. For consistency, the requirements have been extended to cover controllers of all authorised persons incorporated in or formed under the law of any part of the United Kingdom and not just those persons which are included in the scope of the single market directives. This Part does not place notification requirements on persons who exercise control over authorised persons by virtue of their position in that firm or in a

parent firm, for example as a director or chief executive. Such people may, however, need to be approved by the Authority under Part V of the Act.

Section 178: ***Obligation to notify the Authority***

350. This section imposes a requirement on persons who propose to acquire control (or acquire an additional kind of control) or increase their control over a UK authorised person to give the Authority a "notice of control" informing them of their intentions. What constitutes "control" and a "kind of control" for these purposes is described in section 179. The circumstances in which a person is taken to "increase" their control are set out in section 180.

351. *Subsection (2)* provides for passive acquirers of control. These are persons who acquire control without themselves taking any action, for example, through inheriting a large number of shares. A passive acquirer may not be able to notify the Authority in advance, but under this subsection, they must do so within fourteen days of first becoming aware that they have acquired the control.

352. A person who is required by *subsection (1)* to notify the Authority of his proposal to acquire or increase control is also required by *subsection (3)* to make a further notification when the acquisition or increase has taken place.

353. *Subsection (4)* defines the range of authorised persons with whose control this Part is concerned. In line with single market directive requirements this is limited to authorised persons incorporated in or formed under the law of any part of the United Kingdom, "UK authorised persons". This is because under the single market directives, the supervision of those who have control is subject to home State regulation. The requirements do however cover all classes of UK authorised persons and not just those included in the scope of the single market directives.

Section 179: ***Acquiring control***

354. This section defines the circumstances in which a person acquires control and is therefore subject to the obligation to notify the Authority under section 178(1)(a) or (b).

355. A person may acquire control either directly via a shareholding or voting power in the UK authorised person itself, or indirectly via a shareholding or voting power in a parent of the UK authorised person. This is required by the single market directives.

356. *Subsection (3)* provides that for the purposes of determining whether a person has acquired control, the percentage shareholding or voting power is aggregated with that of their associates as defined in section 422. This means, for example, that where a firm has a holding of 5 per cent of the shares in a UK authorised person and one of its subsidiaries has a holding of 7 per cent of the shares in the same UK authorised person, the firm will be required to notify the Authority.

357. *Subsection (4)* sets out what constitutes a "kind" of control. A person who has control of one kind would be required under section 178 to notify the Authority again were they to acquire control of a different kind either as well as, or instead of, the control they had before.

Section 180: ***Increasing control***

358. This section sets out the circumstances in which an increase in a person's control causes them to be subject to the obligation to notify the Authority under section 178(1)(c). These are that a person's shareholding or voting power must cross one of the thresholds set out in *subsection (2)*, or they must become a parent of the UK authorised person. These thresholds are determined largely by the single market directives.

Section 181: ***Reducing control***

359. This section sets out the circumstances in which a reduction in a person's control causes them to be subject to the obligation to notify the Authority under section 190. These are that a person's shareholding or voting power must cross one of the thresholds set out in *subsection (2)*, or they must cease to be a parent of the UK authorised person. The level of these thresholds is as for an increase in control and again they are determined largely by the single market directives.

Section 182: ***Notification***

360. This section concerns the procedure to be followed when notifying the Authority. It specifies that the Authority may indicate the information and documents that must be supplied in support of a notification.

361. *Subsection (2)* confers a power on the Authority to require persons giving a notice of control to provide the Authority with such additional information as the Authority may reasonably considers necessary to determine the application.

Section 183: ***Duty of Authority in relation to notice of control***

362. This section gives the Authority up to three months from the date it receives a completed notice to determine whether to approve the application or issue a warning notice indicating that it is proposing to object to the acquisition of, or increase in, control.

363. *Subsection (2)* imposes a requirement on the Authority to consult home State competent authorities when required to do so by regulations made by the Treasury. The nature of this requirement is determined by the single market directives.

Section 184: ***Approval of acquisition of control***

364. The Authority is obliged by this section to notify the applicant without delay if it gives its approval.

365. If the Authority fails to indicate its approval or to issue a warning notice within three months, *subsection (2)* provides that the applicant is to be treated for the purposes of the Part as having been approved.

366. As a result of *subsection (3)*, the approval is valid for a year, unless the Authority notifies the person intending to acquire control of a another time period. If the person does not acquire the control in that period, a fresh application is required.

Section 185: ***Conditions attached to approval***

367. This section concerns the ability of the Authority to make its approval subject to the imposition of conditions on the applicant. The Authority is able to impose such conditions as it considers desirable, having regard to its duty under section 41 to ensure that, in general, the threshold conditions will continue to be met in relation to the UK authorised person subject to the control concerned.

368. If the Authority imposes conditions, *subsections (3) and (4)* require it to issue the person with a warning notice and a decision notice. The person has a right to refer the matter to the Tribunal.

369. Under *subsection (5)*, persons on whom conditions are imposed may apply to the Authority to have the conditions varied or cancelled. The Authority may itself cancel a condition.

370. The Authority may serve a notice of objection on persons who breach any conditions imposed by this section. This is provided for in section 187.

Section 186: ***Objection to acquisition of control***

371. This section gives the Authority the power to object to the acquisition of new or additional control, or to an increase in control.

372. The Authority can object to a person acquiring or increasing their control where it is not satisfied that the approval requirements set out in *subsection (2)* are met.

373. *Subsection (4)* confers a duty on the Authority to notify the applicant if it considers that the conditions for approval would be met if the applicant took or refrained from taking a particular step.

Section 187: ***Objection to existing control***

374. This section provides the Authority with the power to object to an existing controller if it is satisfied that the approval requirements are not met or that a condition imposed under section 185 has been breached. The Authority may also object to a person who acquired or increased control without notifying the Authority in the required manner.

Section 188: ***Notices of objection under** section 187**: procedure***

375. This section sets out the process by which the Authority can object under section 187 to an existing controller. If the Authority wishes to object to a controller, it is obliged to give him a warning notice.

376. *Subsection (2)* has the effect that the Authority must comply with any requirements prescribed by the Treasury with respect to the consultation of other competent authorities outside the UK before it gives a warning notice. The Treasury will exercise this power to ensure that effect is given to requirements imposed by the single market directives to consult home State competent authorities.

Section 189: ***Improperly acquired shares***

377. This section makes provision enabling the Authority to restrict rights deriving from shares in the case of persons who continue to hold shares in breach of a notice of objection. It is a requirement of the single market directives that these powers should be available.

378. The Authority also has the option of applying to the court for an order directing the sale of shares under *subsection (3)*. If shares are sold in this way, *subsection (6)* provides that the proceeds (net of the costs of the sale) will be paid, via the court, to persons beneficially interested in them.

379. *Subsection (7)* provides that the powers in this section may only be exercised in relation to shares acquired in breach of a notice of objection or in contravention of a condition imposed by the Authority, and not to any other shares held by the person or his associates.

Section 190: ***Notification***

380. This section concerns notification of reductions in, and cessations of, control, whether or not the reduction or cessation is intentional.

381. Under *subsection (1)* a person who proposes to reduce the control that they have over a UK authorised person, or to cease to have any control, must notify the Authority that that is their intention. The circumstances in which a reduction in control triggers this notification requirement are set out in section 181. A person required to notify the Authority under this subsection must, under *subsection (3)*, notify the Authority again when the proposed reduction or cessation of control actually occurs.

382. *Subsection (2)* requires persons whose control is reduced, or ceases, without themselves taking any action, to notify the Authority within 14 days of becoming aware of the reduction or cessation.

383. *Subsection (4)* sets out various requirements in relation to the notices given pursuant to this section.

384. The Authority has no power to make any objection in these circumstances but it is an offence to fail to give the necessary notification.

Section 191: Offences under this Part

385. This section sets out the offences in relation to this Part.

386. *Subsections (1) and (2)* provide that it is an offence not to notify the Authority in accordance with the requirements in this Part when acquiring, increasing, reducing or ceasing to have control over a UK authorised person.

387. *Subsections (3)* and *(4)* provide that where proper notification has been given, it is an offence to carry out a proposal before the Authority has given its approval or, where it has issued a warning notice, before it has decided whether to follow the warning notice with a notice of objection.

388. A person guilty of any of the above offences is liable on summary conviction to a fine not exceeding level 5 on the standard scale, currently £5,000.

389. It is also an offence, under *subsection (5)*, to acquire control in contravention of a notice of objection. This is a more serious offence and a person guilty of it may be convicted on indictment to imprisonment for a term of up to two years and to a fine. There are lesser fines on summary conviction. The penalties are set out in *subsections (7)* and *(8)*, and include provision for a daily fine if the offence continues.

390. S*ubsection (9)* provides a defence for those who are prosecuted for failing to notify the Authority of their influence. The defence is available if a person can show that he was unaware of the act or circumstance by virtue of which the duty to notify the Authority arose. In these circumstances, the person must notify the Authority within 14 days subsequently of becoming aware. Failure to do so is a criminal offence, the penalty on summary conviction being a fine not exceeding level 5 on the standard scale, currently £5,000.

Section 192: Power to change definitions of control etc.

391. This section gives the Treasury power to amend by order certain definitions in this Part and others which are relevant to it, and to provide for exemption from the obligation to notify increases or reductions in control under sections 178 and 190.

392. The Treasury may alter the cases in which a person is said to acquire control as set out in section 179, and therefore it also has a power to change the definition of controller in section 422 to ensure the two remain aligned. The Treasury may also alter the thresholds the crossing of which triggers the requirements in this Part to notify an increase or decrease in control. This power is necessary to give effect to any future change in the single market directive requirements for controllers of UK authorised persons who are not currently covered by the single market directives.

Part Xiii: Incoming Firms: Intervention by Authority

393. This Part confers power on the Authority and, in certain cases, the DGFT to intervene in the business of EEA and Treaty firms who are, or have been, authorised by virtue of Schedules 3 and 4. These firms are referred to in the Part as "incoming firms". This power, which is referred to as the power of intervention, does not apply in respect of persons who are authorised solely by virtue of having a permission under Part IV. Nor

does it apply in respect of the additional Part IV permissions that may be held by incoming firms. The Part sets out the grounds on which the power is exercisable and the procedures for exercising it.

Section 194: ***General grounds on which power of intervention is exercisable***

394. This section sets out the grounds on which the Authority may exercise its power of intervention. The 4 grounds are:

- where it appears to the Authority that there has been, or is likely to be, some contravention of a rule or other requirement imposed by the Authority in accordance with the division of responsibility between home and host State under the appropriate single market directive;
- where it appears to the Authority that the authorised person has knowingly or recklessly misled the Authority;
- where it appears to the Authority that it is desirable to exercise the powers in order to protect customers or potential customers; or
- where the incoming EEA firm is carrying on consumer credit business in the United Kingdom under their passport and the DGFT has informed the Authority that the person has done any of the things listed in section 25(2) of the CCA 1974. These are factors to be taken into account by the DGFT in deciding whether a person is fit and proper to hold a consumer credit licence, and they cover contraventions of that Act, offences involving fraud, dishonesty or violence, practising racial or other forms of discrimination, and engaging in deceitful, oppressive, unfair or improper business practices.

Section 195: ***Exercise of power in support of overseas regulator***

395. This section enables the Authority to exercise its intervention power at the request of, or for the purpose of assisting, an overseas regulatory authority ("ORA"). The Authority may exercise its powers under this section whether or not the grounds set out in the previous section are met. Authorities in other EEA States who are competent authorities under the single market directives are automatically ORAs. Other overseas authorities, from the EEA or elsewhere, which have functions equivalent to those set out in *subsection (4)* are also ORAs.

396. When the Authority receives a request from an EEA competent authority, it must consider whether it is obliged to exercise the powers under the relevant directive. In other cases, the Authority may exercise its discretion, taking account of the factors listed in *subsection (6)*.

397. Under*subsection (7)* the Authority may make its use of its powers conditional on the ORA making an appropriate contribution toward the cost of taking the action.

Section 196: ***The power of intervention***

398. This section provides that the nature and extent of the Authority's power of intervention are the same as the power to vary a permission or impose a requirement under Part IV.

Section 197: ***Procedure on exercise of power of intervention***

399. This section sets out the procedure the Authority must follow when it proposes to exercise its power of intervention against incoming firms under this Part. This is the same written notice procedure as described in relation to section 53.

Section 198: ***Power to apply to the court for injunction in respect of certain overseas insurance companies***

400. Under this section the Authority may act on behalf of an insurance authority in another EEA member State by applying to the courts for an injunction, or in Scotland an interdict, to freeze assets held in the United Kingdom by an insurer from that member State.

401. The power implements article 20(5) of the 1st Non-Life Directive, relating to general insurance, and article 24(5) of the 1st Life Directive, relating to long-term insurance. *Subsection (1)* limits use of the power to where it is in accordance with those provisions, which means that it is exercisable where the firm's home State authority has asked the Authority to prohibit the free disposal of assets of that firm and has confirmed that:

- the firm has failed to comply with the requirements of article 15 of the 1st Non-Life Directive or article 17 of the 1st Life Directive;
- the solvency margin of the firm has fallen below the minimum required by article 16(3) of the 1st Non-Life Directive or article 19 of the 1st Life Directive; or
- the solvency margin of the firm has fallen below the guarantee fund as defined in article 17 of the 1st Non-Life Directive or article 20 of the 1st Life Directive.

Section 199: ***Additional procedure for EEA firms in certain cases***

402. This section imposes an additional procedure to be followed in some circumstances where the Authority proposes to use its intervention power against an EEA firm. This procedure applies where the EEA firm has contravened a requirement imposed by the Authority pursuant to host State functions under the relevant single market directive.

403. First, the Authority must require the firm to remedy the situation. If the firm fails to do so, the Authority must request the firm's home State regulator to take appropriate measures to ensure the firm remedies the situation and inform the Authority of the measures it proposes to take (or why it does not propose to take any measures). Only if the Authority considers that the measures that the home State regulator has taken are inadequate, or if no action has been taken by that regulator, may it exercise its powers.

404. However, where the Authority decides it needs to act urgently it may do so before it has required the firm to remedy the situation and either before it requests the home State regulator to act or, having already made a request, before it is satisfied that the home State regulator is not going to take adequate action. But if the Authority takes urgent action in this way, it must inform the European Commission and must comply with any direction from the Commission to rescind or vary the requirements imposed.

Section 200: ***Rescission and variation of requirements***

405. Either on its own initiative or at the request of the authorised person who is subject to a requirement under this Part, the Authority may rescind or vary such a requirement. The procedure under section 197 applies to a variation on the Authority's own initiative. The warning notice and decision notice procedure applies where the Authority proposes to refuse to rescind or vary a requirement on request. Agreement to a request for rescission or variation can be granted by written notice as with the grant of other forms of application under the Act.

Section 201: ***Effect of certain requirements on other persons***

406. Where the power of intervention is used to impose a restriction on the type mentioned in section 48 (an assets requirement), the restriction has the same effect as if it had been imposed under Part IV. This means that the provisions of section 48 apply, including

the provisions about assets held by a third party such as a bank, and about the transfer of assets to a trustee approved by the Authority.

Section 202: Contravention of a requirement imposed under this Part

407. This section makes clear that a contravention of a requirement imposed under this Part does not constitute an offence or result in any transaction being void or unenforceable. It also confers on the Treasury a power to prescribe in regulations the circumstances in which a person may have a right of action as a result of a breach of a requirement imposed under this Part. Otherwise no such right of action will result from a contravention.

Section 203: Powers to prohibit the carrying on of Consumer Credit Act business

408. Under the Act, EEA firms may, on the basis of their home State authorisation, be automatically authorised to carry on the types of activity covered by the passport under the various single market directives. Two of these directives include lending in their listed activities, which encompasses consumer credit business regulated in the United Kingdom under the CCA 1974. This means that EEA firms may carry on consumer credit business without having to apply to the DGFT for a consumer credit licence and they are therefore not subject to the DGFT's powers under the CCA 1974.

409. This section, along with section 204, confers on the DGFT separate powers to restrict or prohibit the carrying on, or the purported carrying on, of consumer credit business in the United Kingdom under the relevant directives if the firm or any of its employees has done any of the things listed in section 25(2)(a) to (d) of the CCA 1974. That is, if they have:

- committed any offence involving fraud, dishonesty or violence;
- contravened any provision made by or under the CCA 1974, or by or under any other enactment regulating the provision of credit to individuals or other transactions with individuals;
- practised discrimination on grounds of sex, colour, race or ethnic or national origins in, or in connection with, the carrying on of any business; or
- engaged in business practices appearing to the DGFT to be deceitful or oppressive, or otherwise unfair or improper (whether unlawful or not).

410. Contravention of a restriction or prohibition is a criminal offence and contravention of a restriction is also grounds for imposing a prohibition. Schedule 16 sets out the procedure the DGFT must follow when imposing prohibitions or restrictions. This procedure follows that generally applicable in the CCA 1974 rather than in the other provisions of this Act.

Part Xiv: Disciplinary Measures

411. This Part gives the Authority powers to issue public statements or impose financial penalties in response to contraventions of rules or other requirements by authorised persons.

Section 205: Public censure

412. This gives the Authority the power to make a public statement concerning a contravention by an authorised person of any requirement imposed directly by the Act or under it, for example through the Authority exercising its rule-making power.

*Section 206: **Financial penalties***

413. This enables the Authority to impose a financial penalty where it establishes that there has been a contravention by an authorised person of any requirement imposed by or under the Act.

*Section 207: **Proposal to take disciplinary measures***

414. This section requires the Authority to issue a warning notice where it proposes to make a public statement about an alleged contravention or impose a penalty. The notice must include the statement the Authority proposes to make or the amount of the proposed penalty.

*Section 208: **Decision notice***

415. If having issued a warning notice, and heard any representations, the Authority decides at the end of the relevant period to proceed with the public statement or penalty, it must issue a decision notice. This should also set out the terms of the proposed statement or the amount of the proposed fine (either of which may change in response to any representations made).

416. The authorised person has a right to have the matter referred to the Tribunal, in accordance with the provisions of Part IX of the Act. No further action can be taken by the Authority during the period in which the person has the right to have the matter referred to the Tribunal or, where the matter has been referred, until the Tribunal hearing and any subsequent appeal have run their course.

*Section 209: **Publication***

417. If, having followed the appropriate procedures, the Authority decides to make a public statement under section 205, this section provides that it must send a copy of the statement to the authorised person concerned and to any third parties to whom it copied the decision notice.

*Section 210: **Statements of policy***

418. This section requires the Authority to prepare and publish guidance on its policy concerning the imposition of penalties under section 206 and the level of those penalties. Under *subsection (7),* the Authority must have regard to this published guidance when determining the level of penalties.

*Section 211: **Statements of policy: procedure***

419. This section requires the Authority to follow certain procedures when it issues a policy statement under section 210. The procedures include a requirement to consult on its proposals.

Part Xv: the Financial Services Compensation Scheme

420. This Part of the Act provides for a single Financial Services Compensation Scheme, established by the Authority and managed by an independent scheme manager. It gives the Authority powers to specify the regulated activities covered by the scheme.

421. The purpose of the compensation scheme is to compensate customers who suffer loss in various circumstances as a consequence of the inability of an authorised person to meet its liabilities. The scheme is not, other than in cases of the insolvency of an authorised person, intended to provide compensation for a regulatory breach (for example the mis-selling of investments), where the liability would remain with the authorised firm.

Section 212: The scheme manager

422. This section requires the Authority to establish a company to manage the scheme and sets requirements as to the company's constitution, including that the chairman should be appointed by the Authority with the approval of the Treasury and that board members should act independently of the Authority.

Section 213: The compensation scheme

423. This section imposes certain requirements about the Authority's rules establishing the scheme. It also makes it clear that customers may be eligible to make a claim against an authorised person even if the claim arises in relation to an activity for which that authorised person did not have permission. A claim relating to an appointed representative who is an exempt person by virtue of section 39 may also qualify under the scheme. Claims would not, however, be eligible if they related to regulated activities carried on by a person who should be authorised but is not.

424. *Subsection (3)(b)* provides for the scheme manager to levy authorised persons to cover both the costs of compensation and its administrative costs.

425. *Subsection (5)* requires the scheme manager when setting the levy to seek, so far as is practicable, to avoid cross-subsidy between sectors.

426. *Subsection (10)* allows the Treasury to prescribe categories of persons authorised to carry on regulated activities in the United Kingdom under passporting arrangements that will only participate in the scheme if they elect to do so. This allows the Treasury to ensure that, while membership of the scheme is generally compulsory for authorised persons carrying on relevant activities, it remains compatible with UK obligations under EC directives which make rules about the extent to which EEA firms can be required to join compensation schemes other than their home State scheme.

Section 214: General

427. This section clarifies the scope of the Authority's power to make scheme rules.

428. *Subsection (1)* provides, in particular, that the scheme may consist of a number of different compensation funds, for which levies can be raised from different sectors of the industry and different rules may be made as to the level of and eligibility for compensation.

429. *Subsections (2) to (4)* enable the scheme to limit the eligibility of claimants according to a number of different factors, including where the event took place or where the claimant resides.

430. *Subsection (6)* confers on the scheme manager a power to enter into arrangements with schemes established in other countries outside the EEA. Where, for example, a US firm does business in the United Kingdom and the level of compensation under the US scheme is lower than in the United Kingdom, the firm would be able to become a member of the UK scheme for the purposes of topping-up its cover. If the firm was unable to meet its liabilities, claimants might have a claim against both the US and the UK schemes. This power would in turn enable the UK scheme to enter into an arrangement with the US scheme to avoid the need for the claimant to submit a claim to both schemes. It is possible to make reciprocal arrangements under the power in *subsection (1)(k)*.

Section 215: Rights of the scheme in relevant person's insolvency

431. *Subsection (1)* enables the Authority to make provision about the effect of a payment of compensation under the scheme on the rights and obligations arising out of the claim against a relevant person in respect of which the payment was made. This allows the Authority to make provision for the rights of the claimant to be transferred to

the scheme manager, which would enable the scheme manager to seek to recoup the costs of paying compensation from the firm in question without increasing the firm's liabilities. *Subsection (2)* provides that any right of recovery conferred on the scheme manager under *subsection (1)* cannot exceed the claimant's original rights.

Section 216: Continuity of long-term insurance policies

432. The special nature of long-term insurance means that should an insurer go into liquidation, a simple payment of compensation may not necessarily be enough to enable policyholders to find alternative cover. This would be a problem especially where a person had developed health problems since taking out the original policy. The purpose of this section is to enable the Authority to include in the scheme rules a requirement for the scheme manager to seek to transfer the business of a failing insurer, so far as it relates to contracts of long-term insurance, to another company or to secure the issue of substitute policies by another insurer.

Section 217: Insurers in financial difficulties

433. The special features of long-term (or "life") business are noted above. But even general insurance business (for example car or product liability insurance) can result in claims arising from events which may have happened several years earlier. This long tail of claims means that it can be difficult to crystalise the liabilities of an insurer in liquidation. The administration of insurance claims is costly and the delays for policyholders can be substantial while a liquidator seeks to work out the level of payments that can be made to creditors.

434. Accordingly, this section allows the Authority to make provision for the scheme manager to give assistance to an authorised person with permission to effect and carry out contracts of insurance in financial difficulties, either by transferring the that person's business, so far as it relates to contracts of insurance, to another insurer, or by enabling the continuance of that business by another insurer. Before using this power, which is potentially of substantial benefit to policyholders, the scheme manager must be satisfied that payments to the firm should not materially benefit other persons such as shareholders or company directors. It must also be satisfied that these measures would not cost more than the costs of compensation if the firm were allowed to go into default.

Section 219: Scheme manager's power to require information

435. The efficient settlement of claims will sometimes require the scheme to obtain information from a variety of sources. This section provides the scheme manager with powers to require the provision of specified information that it considers necessary in order to be able to assess claims. Information may be required from the authorised person, or from a person who was knowingly involved in the events giving rise to the claim.

Section 220: Scheme manager's power to inspect information held by liquidator etc

436. This section allows the scheme manager to inspect information held by the liquidator, administrator or trustee in bankruptcy of an insolvent relevant person. The scheme manager is only allowed to inspect documents rather than require them to be produced, which means that the cost of copying documents will be borne by the scheme and not by the liquidator. This should reduce costs to the liquidator, administrator or trustee in bankruptcy. The section does not apply to the Official Receiver or his Scotland and Northern Ireland counterparts (as to which see section 224).

Section 221: Powers of court where information required

437. This section provides that, where a person fails to comply with a requirement for information under section 219 or to permit documents to be inspected under section 220,

this may be certified to the court, which may deal with the person as though he were in contempt.

*Section 222: **Statutory immunity***

438. This section provides immunity for the scheme manager, and its staff from actions for damages, except where they act in bad faith or where damages are sought under section 6(1) of the Human Rights Act 1998.

*Section 223: **Management expenses***

439. This section ensures that the scheme may only recover from levies management expenses up to a certain limit. The limit must be set before the scheme includes management expenses in its calculations of the levies.

Part Xvi: the Ombudsman Scheme

440. This Part of the Act provides for the creation of a single, compulsory ombudsman scheme for the resolution of disputes between authorised firms and their customers. It provides for the detailed operation of the scheme to be determined largely by rules made by the Authority on which it is required to consult in accordance with the requirements under Part X.

*Section 225: **The scheme and the scheme operator***

441. This section makes clear that the object of the scheme is to resolve disputes involving consumers quickly and with minimum formality. The operator of the scheme must be a body corporate.

*Section 226: **Compulsory jurisdiction***

442. This section requires firms authorised by the Authority to submit to the jurisdiction of the scheme. The scheme's compulsory jurisdiction may only be applied to persons who were authorised at the time the activity to which the complaint relates was carried out, and the rules must have been in force at that time. The Authority is to make rules determining which activities of authorised persons fall within the compulsory jurisdiction. These activities must either be regulated activities as specified by the Treasury under section 22 or other activities which are not regulated, but could be made regulated activities under that section. The Authority is free not to include certain activities, for example kinds of professional business where it is unlikely that retail customers would ever be involved.

443. If an activity is included in the compulsory jurisdiction of the scheme, the ombudsman can consider all disputes arising from the carrying on of that activity by the authorised person. For example, were accepting deposits specified as an activity covered by the compulsory jurisdiction of the scheme, the ombudsman could consider all disputes arising from the operation of a bank account, such as the withdrawal of money from a cash machine, or a stopped cheque.

444. The section also sets the circumstances in which a complaint can be dealt with: namely, that the complainant meets the relevant eligibility criteria (set by the Authority) and has asked the ombudsman to consider the case. The scheme is not able to deal with complaints made by authorised persons, except in circumstances specified in the rules.

*Section 227: **Voluntary jurisdiction***

445. Firms can join the ombudsman scheme, on a voluntary basis, under the voluntary jurisdiction where they are not authorised by the Authority or in respect of activities falling outside the scope of the compulsory jurisdiction. However, the scheme's voluntary jurisdiction rules can only relate to activities which are subject, or could be

made subject, to the compulsory jurisdiction rules. The voluntary jurisdiction can be applied to authorised persons where a complaint relates to an activity which could be, but has not been, made subject to compulsory jurisdiction rules.

446. Voluntary jurisdiction rules can be made by the scheme operator with the approval of the Authority. The rules will also define which complainants are eligible.

Section 228: ***Determination under the compulsory jurisdiction***

447. The ombudsman will make a decision about the complaint on the basis of what he considers is fair and reasonable in the circumstances. The scheme operator has the power under paragraph 14 of Schedule 17 to specify the matters that can be taken into account when determining what is fair and reasonable. The ombudsman must make a written statement of his reasons for the decision, and must also require the claimant to accept or reject the decision by a specified date. If the complainant accepts the ombudsman's decision, then it is binding on both the complainant and the respondent.

Section 229: ***Awards***

448. If a complaint under the compulsory jurisdiction is determined in favour of the complainant, the respondent may be ordered to pay compensation up to a maximum limit which may be set by the Authority. The limit may be different for different kinds of complaint. The Authority may specify a particular limit for compensation in respect of non-financial loss or damage. The ombudsman can only make a binding award up to the limit set by the Authority, but he may recommend a greater amount as fair compensation. The respondent may also be ordered to take steps to rectify the matter complained of, and this can be enforced through the courts by the complainant if necessary.

Section 230: ***Costs***

449. This section allows the scheme operator to make rules concerning the costs which can be awarded by the ombudsman. These rules are subject to certain constraints. Where a complaint is settled in favour of the complainant, the rules can allow the firm concerned to be required to meet the costs of both the complainant and the scheme operator. A complainant could only ever be required to meet the costs of the scheme, and then only if the scheme operator had made rules to allow for such awards and the ombudsman believed that the complainant's conduct has been improper or unreasonable, or they had been responsible for an unreasonable delay. The section also makes provision for recovery of costs by the scheme operator.

Section 231: ***Ombudsman's power to require information***

450. The efficient settlement of complaints under the compulsory jurisdiction will sometimes require the scheme to obtain information from the parties to the dispute. This section provides the scheme operator with powers to require parties to the complaint to provide specified information which it considers necessary for the fair determination of the complaint. It is not expected that these powers will be used on a routine basis. The Authority will also have powers to make rules requiring authorised persons to co-operate with the scheme. It will be in the interests of the complainant to co-operate.

Section 232: ***Powers of court where information required***

451. This section provides that, if a person fails to comply with a requirement to provide information made under section 231, the matter may be certified to the court, which may deal with the person as if they were in contempt.

Section 233: Data protection

452. This section inserts new subsection (4A) into section 31 of the Data Protection Act 1998. This is needed to ensure that the scheme operator does not have to disclose information it has obtained when considering a complaint brought under the ombudsman scheme if disclosure would prejudice the performance of its functions.

Section 234: Industry funding

453. This section provides for the Authority to be able to levy fees on authorised persons to meet both the costs of establishing the scheme and the costs of running the compulsory jurisdiction. The costs of the voluntary jurisdiction will be met by fees set as part of the voluntary jurisdiction rules.

Part Xvii: Collective Investment Schemes

454. This Part comprises six chapters concerning collective investment schemes, including unit trusts, open-ended investment companies ("oeics") and overseas schemes. It includes provisions relating to the authorisation of schemes, their trustees, managers and operators and also to the rules applicable to them. The Part also makes provision for overseas collective investment schemes which may be promoted in the United Kingdom:

- Chapter I provides the relevant definitions for this Part. It also gives the Treasury the power to specify by order that certain arrangements will not constitute a collective investment scheme.
- Chapter II prohibits authorised persons from promoting participation in a collective investment scheme unless an exemption applies. Whilst the provisions broadly continue the prohibition on authorised persons promoting collective investment schemes under the FS Act 1986, changes have been made to reflect the new financial promotion regime set out in section 21.
- Chapter III contains the provisions relating to authorised unit trust schemes. These broadly follow the provisions of the FS Act 1986, although the Authority is to be given the power to approve changes to an authorised unit trust's investment and borrowing powers. There are also provisions to allow for rule waivers and modifications, and to grant operators and trustees of authorised unit trust schemes the right to refer matters to the Tribunal in certain circumstances.
- Chapter IV contains provisions which enable the Treasury broadly to continue the regime for oeics, and to make regulations concerning the establishment and regulation of other forms of oeic in the United Kingdom. Under the FS Act 1986, oeics which are incorporated and authorised in the United Kingdom must invest solely in transferable securities. The Act will allow the Treasury to make regulations concerning the creation and operation of a wider range of authorised oeics, so that they can invest in assets other than transferable securities. The Treasury may also, under the relevant provisions, make regulations concerning the incorporation of unauthorised oeics. This might, for example, be done in order to allow the formation of common investment funds for charitable purposes, or in the context of ethical investments.
- Chapter V broadly carries forward provisions of the FS Act 1986 and allows three kinds of overseas scheme to be "recognised" and marketed in the United Kingdom. First, schemes constituted in other member states which meet particular requirements; second, schemes authorised in designated territories; and third, schemes constituted in other territories, but which are individually recognised.
- Chapter VI sets out the powers of investigation which will apply in relation to authorised unit trust and overseas schemes. It is intended that the principal

provisions concerning investigations of oeics will be set out in the proposed Treasury regulations under Chapter IV.

Chapter I: Interpretation

Section 236: Open-ended investment companies

455. This section defines an open-ended investment company. This is done by reference to a "property" and an "investment" test (set out in *subsections (2) and (3)* respectively). Both tests must be satisfied in order for a corporate body to meet the definition of an open-ended investment company. The "property" test is carried over from the definition in section 75(8)(a) of the FS Act 1986.

456. The "investment" test is framed by reference to a hypothetical reasonable investor's expectations, were he to participate in the scheme. A reasonable investor should expect to realise his investment within a reasonable period, and expect that the way in which this would be done would be calculated by reference to the value of the scheme property. In determining whether this condition is satisfied, certain actual or potential redemptions of his holdings are to be ignored, including those under certain provisions of the Companies Act and corresponding provisions in EEA states. Under *subsection (4)(d)*, the Treasury may by order designate provisions in non-EEA states under which redemptions may be made and which may also be left out of the account.

457. *Subsection (5)* contains a Treasury order-making power to amend the definition of an open-ended investment company for the purposes of Part XVII.

Chapter II: Restrictions on promotion

Section 238: Restrictions on promotion

458. This section contains the basic marketing prohibition and some exemptions from it. The main exemption is for schemes which are marketed other than to the general public. Other exemptions include promotions made in respect of authorised unit trust schemes, authorised oeics and recognised overseas schemes. The marketing prohibition applies to communications which originate outside the United Kingdom if the communication is capable of having an effect in the United Kingdom.

459. *Subsection (6)* enables the Treasury by order to specify circumstances in which the *subsection (1)* prohibition does not apply. For incoming promotions, *subsection (7)* makes it clear that it will be possible to make exemptions dealing with promotions originating outside the United Kingdom even if they are capable of having an effect in the United Kingdom. Thus, *subsection (7)* makes clear that the order-making power in *subsection (6)* enables the Treasury to adjust the scope of the restriction on promotion of collective investment schemes by authorised persons to take full account of international and technological developments.

460. The term "promotion otherwise than to the general public" is amplified in *subsection (10)* and includes promotions which are designed, so far as possible, to reduce the risk of participation by persons for whom it would be unsuitable. The prohibition on marketing to the general public will not therefore necessarily be breached if a promotion is inadvertently received by a member of the general public.

Section 239: Single property schemes

461. A single property scheme is, broadly, a collective investment scheme which relates to a single building or a group of buildings managed as a single enterprise. This section gives the Treasury power to make regulations exempting the promotion of participation in single property schemes to the general public from the prohibition in section 238. If the Treasury make regulations under this section, the Authority may then make rules

imposing duties on the operator and trustee or depositary of schemes exempted under the regulations.

*Section 240: **Restriction on approval of promotion***

462. This is a new provision designed to prevent an authorised person from approving a financial promotion under section 21 if the authorised person would not himself be permitted to make the communication under section 238.

*Section 241: **Actions for damages***

463. If an authorised person contravenes a requirement under section 238 or 240, a private person, and other persons falling within such categories as may be prescribed in regulations made by the Treasury, who suffers loss as a result may claim damages.

Chapter III: Authorised unit trust schemes

*Section 242: **Applications for authorisation of unit trust schemes***

464. Applications for an order declaring a unit trust scheme to be authorised must be made to the Authority by the manager and trustee of the scheme. The manager and trustee must be different persons. The section gives the Authority broad scope to determine the form and content of the application, including further information to be contained in it.

*Section 243: **Authorisation orders***

465. If the conditions referred to in the section are met, the Authority may make an authorisation order declaring a unit trust scheme to be authorised. The conditions reflect certain requirements specified in the UCITS Directive which establishes a passporting regime whereby certain types of authorised collective investment scheme established in one EEA State may generally be entitled to equivalent authorisation in others. The section includes requirements that:

- the manager and trustee must be bodies corporate which are independent of each other and incorporated in the United Kingdom or another EEA State;
- they must be authorised persons holding the appropriate permissions;
- the scheme must comply with the requirements of the trust scheme rules (referred to at section 247, below); and
- participants must be able to have their units redeemed at a price related to the net asset value of the scheme property or be able to sell their units on an exchange at a similar price.

*Section 244: **Determination of applications***

466. This section sets out the time limits within which applications should be determined (and specifies that completed applications shall be determined within six months). Applicants may withdraw their application at any time before the Authority makes a determination.

*Section 245: **Procedure when refusing an application***

467. If the Authority wishes to refuse an application, it must issue each of the manager and trustee with a warning notice. Either the manager or the trustee may refer a refusal to the Tribunal.

*Section 246: **Certificates***

468. If an authorised unit trust scheme meets with the requirements of the UCITS Directive, the manager or trustee of the scheme can request that the Authority issue a certificate to that effect. The certificate will be needed if the authorised unit trust scheme is to passport into other European jurisdictions.

*Section 247: **Trust scheme rules***

469. This section permits the Authority to make rules (known as "trust scheme rules") concerning the constitution, management and operation of authorised unit trust schemes. These cover broadly the same matters as constitution and management regulations under section 81 of the FS Act 1986, but without the arrangements under that legislation whereby the Treasury retained a degree of control over certain constitution and management matters (such as the investment and borrowing powers of authorised unit trusts). The Authority has direct responsibility for these matters under this section.

470. The trust scheme rules are binding on the manager, trustee and participants independently of any provisions contained in the trust deed. Participants can seek to enforce the trust scheme rules against the manager or trustee as if the rules were provisions contained directly in the trust deed.

471. The Treasury has the power to modify the Authority's rule-making powers if there is a change in the company law relating to the rights of beneficial, but not legal, owners of shares. This would enable the rights of nominee holders in authorised unit trusts to be aligned to those of shareholders in companies should the need arise.

*Section 248: **Scheme particulars rules***

472. These are rules which the Authority may make requiring the manager of an authorised unit trust scheme to give details of the scheme to the Authority and to publish or make available to the public on request certain particulars, including changes, concerning the scheme.

473. The scheme particulars rules can provide for compensation to be paid to certain people (described as "qualifying persons") if they have suffered loss because of an untrue or misleading statement in the particulars or because of an omission from them. Qualifying persons include people who may have a beneficial, but not legal, interest in the scheme (for example, beneficiaries of a trust where the trustees hold units in the scheme).

*Section 249: **Disqualification of auditor for breach of trust scheme rules***

474. The Authority may disqualify an auditor from auditing authorised unit trust schemes or authorised oeics if the auditor does not comply with the trust scheme rules. Warning and decision notice procedures will apply, as well as rights to refer a decision to the Tribunal.

*Section 250: **Modification or waiver of rules***

475. This allows the Authority to modify or waive the application of any of the trust scheme rules or scheme particulars rules in respect of authorised unit trusts. If there is a modification or waiver of rules under this section, certain of the provisions of section 148 (relating to the modification or waiver of various other of the Authority's rules and providing for the circumstances in which waivers or modifications will be granted) will apply.

*Section 251: **Alteration of schemes and changes of manager or trustee***

476. Alterations to an authorised unit trust scheme or a change in the manager or trustee may not take place without the Authority's approval, or the Authority not notifying

its disapproval. New managers or trustees must satisfy the requirements specified in section 243.

*Section 252: **Procedure when refusing approval of change of manager or trustee***

477. If the Authority proposes to refuse to approve the replacement of the trustee or manager, a warning notice must be given. If the Authority proposes to refuse to approve changes to the scheme, warning and decision notice procedures will apply and the matter can be referred to the Tribunal.

*Section 253: **Avoidance of exclusion clauses***

478. As a result of this section, if a trust deed for an authorised unit trust scheme seeks to avoid the manager's or trustee's duty to exercise due care, the deed will be ineffective.

*Section 254: **Revocation of authorisation order otherwise than by consent***

479. The Authority may revoke an order authorising a unit trust in the circumstances specified in the section. These include any of the following situations:

- the manager or trustee has contravened a requirement imposed by the Act or the Authority's rules;
- either of them has given the Authority misleading information;
- the requirements for making an authorisation order (referred to in section 243) are no longer met;
- the scheme has been inactive for 12 months or more; or
- it is desirable in the interests of participants to revoke the scheme's authorisation.

*Section 255: **Procedure***

480. If the Authority wishes to revoke an authorisation order, it must go through the warning and decision notice procedure, giving notice to both the manager and trustee. Either of them may refer the decision to the Tribunal.

*Section 256: **Requests for revocation of authorisation order***

481. The Authority can revoke an authorisation order where the manager or trustee requests it to, but it can also refuse to revoke authorisation where it considers that refusal would be in the interests of participants, or that the public interest requires an investigation before authorisation is revoked. Warning and decision notice procedures will apply and the decision may be referred to the Tribunal.

*Section 257: **Directions***

482. The Authority may give directions requiring the manager of the scheme to cease the issue or redemption of units, or to require the manager and trustee of the scheme to wind it up in the circumstances specified in the section (which are broadly similar to those specified as grounds for revoking a scheme's authorisation under section 254). If a person contravenes a direction under this section, private persons, and others falling within such categories as may be prescribed in regulations made by the Treasury, who suffer loss as a result may be able to bring an action. Once a direction has been given, the Authority may revoke or vary that direction, either of its own accord, or on the application of the manager or trustee.

Section 258: Applications to the court

483. In cases where the Authority is able to give a direction under section 257, it may also apply to the court for an order removing and replacing the manager or the trustee, or simply removing them and appointing an authorised person to wind up the scheme.

Section 259: Procedure in giving directions under section 257 and varying them on Authority's own initiative

484. This section sets out the procedure the Authority must follow when it proposes to give, or on its own initiative vary, a direction in relation to an authorised unit trust scheme under section 257. This is the same written notice procedure as described in relation to section 53, except that in this case separate notices must be given to both the manager and trustee of the scheme. If a notice under this section imposes a requirement for the manager of the scheme to cease issue or redemption of units, it will either give a date when the requirement ends, or else provide for the requirement to continue until a further notice is given. If a notice under this section imposes a requirement to wind up a scheme, the scheme must be wound up either by a date given in the notice or else (if no date is given) as soon as possible.

Section 260: Procedure: refusal to revoke or vary direction

485. If the manager or trustee applies to the Authority for it to revoke or vary a direction given under section 257, but the Authority proposes to refuse to do so, the warning and decision notice procedures will apply. The decision may be referred to the Tribunal.

Section 261: Procedure: revocation of direction and grant of request for variation

486. If the Authority decides to revoke a direction under section 257, or to vary a direction in accordance with a request, it must give written notice of that fact. The Authority may publish information about the revocation or variation of the direction.

Chapter IV: Open-ended investment companies

Section 262: Open-ended investment companies

487. This section creates the broad framework for Treasury regulations relating to the establishment, carrying on, and regulation, of oeics. It provides a wide-ranging and non-exhaustive list of matters which the regulations may provide for. These include imposing criminal liability, conferring functions on the Authority (including rule-making powers and power to waive or modify rules) and power to modify or exclude any statute or rule of law. In particular, the regulations may revoke the existing regulations governing oeics and provide for transitional arrangements for "grandfathering" under those regulations.

Section 263: Amendment of section 716 Companies Act 1985

488. This section amends the Companies Act, so that the prohibition on formation of companies with more than 20 members other than under the Companies Act will not apply to oeics incorporated by virtue of regulations made the by Treasury under section 262.

Chapter V: Recognised overseas schemes

Section 264: Schemes constituted in other EEA States

489. This section relates to the ability of collective investment schemes constituted in other EEA States to passport into the United Kingdom. EEA schemes will be recognised if:

- they satisfy requirements prescribed by Treasury regulations;

- the operator of the scheme gives notice to the Authority of the proposal to invite UK persons to participate in the scheme; and
- the Authority does not give notice that the way in which the invitation is to be made does not comply with the relevant UK law.

Section 265: Representations and references to the Tribunal

490. This section sets out the procedure if the Authority gives notice that it does not consider that the proposed invitations will comply with UK law, and representations are made to the Authority in response. The procedures allow for rights of reference to the Tribunal where the Authority issues a decision notice confirming that the way in which the proposed invitations are to be made does not comply with UK law.

Section 266: Disapplication of rules

491. Rules made by the Authority will not generally apply to the operator, trustee or depositary of a recognised scheme under section 264. The exceptions are financial promotion rules, and rules relating to the maintenance of facilities in the United Kingdom (under section 283(1)).

Section 267: Power of authority to suspend promotion of scheme

492. Although it cannot suspend an EEA scheme's recognition, the Authority can suspend its promotion to the public if it appears that the operator has contravened financial promotion rules. The warning and decision notice procedure will apply and the Authority will be required to notify the scheme's home State authority if it decides to give a direction under this section. The operator will have a right to refer the decision to the Tribunal.

493. Under this section, the Authority may also revoke, as well as vary, a direction suspending the promotion of an EEA scheme, where specified conditions are met.

Section 268: Procedure in giving directions under section 267 and varying them on Authority's own initiative

494. This section establishes the procedure the Authority must follow when it proposes to give, or on its own initiative vary, a direction under section 267 suspending the promotion of a scheme which is recognised under section 264. This is the same written notice procedure as described in relation to section 53 except that the notices in question are to be given to the operator of the scheme concerned. In addition the Authority is required, when giving notice under this section, to inform the competent authorities in the scheme's home State.

Section 269: Procedure on application for variation or revocation of direction

495. This section sets out the procedure the Authority must follow on receipt of an application under section 267(4) or (5) for variation or revocation of a direction suspending the promotion of a scheme which is recognised under section 264. Where an application is granted in full, simple written notice is to be given under *subsection (4)*. The same applies where the Authority decides to revoke a direction on its own initiative under *subsection (5)*. Where the Authority proposes to refuse the application, or proposes to vary the direction in a way other than that requested in the application, the applicant is entitled to receive a warning notice setting out the reasons for the decision, the standard opportunity to make representations, a decision notice and the right to refer the matter to the Tribunal if still aggrieved by the decision. Notices under this section are to be given to the operator of the scheme concerned, but in addition the Authority is required to inform the competent authorities in the scheme's home State.

Section 270: Schemes authorised in designated countries or territories

496. Schemes managed in, and authorised under, the law of non-EEA territories can be recognised under this section. In order to be recognised, the relevant territory needs to be designated by an order made by the Treasury, and the Authority must give its approval to the scheme being recognised. The Treasury may not make an order designating a territory unless it is satisfied that the relevant overseas law under which the scheme is authorised and supervised affords at least equivalent protection to that provided by the UK law on collective investment schemes.

497. In considering whether to make an order designating a country or territory under this section, the Treasury must ask the Authority for a report on the law and practice of the country or territory in question and on any arrangements it has made to co-operate with the authorities there.

Section 271: Procedure

498. If the Authority proposes to refuse to approve a scheme under section 270, it must give the operator a warning notice. The decision notice procedure will apply, and the decision may be referred to the Tribunal.

Section 272: Individually recognised overseas schemes

499. This section allows the Authority to recognise schemes which are not managed in an EEA country or a designated territory.

500. In order to be recognised, the Authority must be satisfied as to various matters, including the adequacy of protection for the participants in the place where the scheme is established, the adequacy of the constitution and management and of the powers and duties of the operator, trustee and depositary (if any), and that those persons are either authorised (with appropriate permissions) or, if not authorised, fit and proper persons. In addition, overseas schemes will only be recognised under this section if they are oeics or schemes where the operator is a body corporate.

Section 273: Matters that may be taken into account

501. This section specifies matters which the Authority can take into account when considering whether the operator, trustee or depository of an individually recognised scheme is fit and proper.

Section 274: Applications for recognition of individual schemes

502. The Authority has broad scope to specify the form and content of applications (which must be made by the operator) and to seek additional information before determining an application.

Section 275: Determination of applications

503. This section sets out the time periods which will apply for the determination of an application. Completed applications are to be determined within six months.

Section 276: Procedure when refusing an application

504. The Authority must go through the warning and decision notice procedure if it proposes to refuse an application. The applicant may refer the refusal to the Tribunal.

Section 277: Alteration of schemes and changes of operator, trustee or depository

505. Changes to the scheme itself cannot be made unless the operator has given notice to the Authority, and the Authority has either approved the proposal, or not notified its disapproval. As for the replacement of the operator, trustee or depositary, at least one

month's notice must be given to the Authority either by the person being replaced, or the person proposing to replace him, but there is no express provision for the Authority to approve or disapprove the replacements.

*Section 278: **Rules as to scheme particulars***

506. The Authority may make rules imposing duties on the operators of recognised schemes which are constituted in designated territories under section 270 or which are individually recognised under section 272. These rules broadly correlate to scheme particulars rules for authorised unit trusts.

*Section 279: **Revocation of recognition***

507. Recognition of schemes constituted in designated territories or individually recognised schemes can be revoked in the circumstances set out in this section. These are broadly similar to the grounds for revocation of an authorisation order under section 254.

*Section 280: **Procedure***

508. If the Authority proposes to revoke recognition under section 279, the warning and decision notice procedure will apply. Notice must be given to the operator, and if any, the trustee and depositary. The decision may be referred to the Tribunal.

*Section 281: **Directions***

509. Instead of proposing to revoke recognition under section 279, the Authority can effectively direct that a scheme's recognition will be suspended.

*Section 282: **Procedure on giving directions under** section 281 **and varying them otherwise than as requested***

510. This section establishes the procedure the Authority must follow when it proposes to give a direction by virtue of its powers of intervention against schemes recognised under sections 270 and 272. This is the same written notice procedure as described in relation to section 53, except that in this case separate notices must be given to both the operator and (if there is one) to the trustee or depository of the scheme.

*Section 283: **Facilities and information in the UK***

511. The Authority may make rules requiring operators of all recognised schemes to maintain facilities in the United Kingdom. It may also require the operator of a recognised scheme to include explanatory information in financial promotions which name the scheme.

Chapter VI: Investigations

*Section 284: **Power to investigate***

512. The Authority or the Secretary of State can appoint a person to carry out investigations into collective investment schemes. The provisions do not generally extend to the investigation of oeics. Provision concerning those investigations can be made in Treasury regulations under section 262.

513. The person carrying out the investigation has powers to investigate other persons or matters where necessary or relevant. The provisions concerning the conduct of investigations set out in section 170 will generally apply and statements made to the investigator may be admissible in proceedings in the circumstances set out in section 174. Persons other than the managers, trustees, operators or depositaries of schemes, or directors of oeics, will not generally be required to disclose information subject to the bankers' duty of confidentiality. The power of entry under section 176

will be available to back up information requirements imposed under this section. The provisions of section 177 will also apply, so that failure to comply with a requirement imposed in connection with an investigation can be certified to a court and falsification or concealment will be an offence.

Part Xviii: Recognised Investment Exchanges and Clearing Houses

514. This Part provides for the regulatory regime for recognised investment exchanges and clearing houses. These recognised bodies are exempt from the need to be authorised. This regime is similar to that under the FS Act 1986.

515. Chapter I of this Part:

- gives the Treasury the power to set the requirements that such bodies have to meet in order to be recognised;
- sets out the application procedures and supervisory arrangements for recognised bodies, including conferring powers to revoke recognition and to direct recognised bodies to take steps to meet the recognition requirements;
- allows the Treasury, jointly with the Secretary of State, to extend special protection from insolvency law to organisations clearing certain non-investment contracts.

516. Chapter II provides for competition scrutiny of recognised bodies. This places a duty on the DGFT, and gives him powers, to investigate and report to the Competition Commission on any significantly adverse effects on competition of these bodies' rules, guidance and practices, or any exploitation of a strong market position. It allows the Treasury, on receipt of a further report from the Commission, to direct, through the Authority, that appropriate changes are made to such rules, guidance or practices. Chapter III disapplies the general domestic competition law as it affects the matters covered by the Act regime. Chapter IV contains definitions of key terms.

Chapter I: Exemption

*Section 285: **Exemption for recognised investment exchanges and clearing houses***

517. *Subsection (1)* defines what is meant by a recognised investment exchange and clearing house.

518. *Subsections (2) and (3)* set out the scope of the exemption for recognised bodies from the need to be authorised in order to carry on regulated activities which it carries on as an exchange or clearing house. Exchanges are also exempt as respects anything they do for the purposes of, or in connection with, the provision of clearing services.

*Section 286: **Qualification for recognition***

519. *Subsection (1)* allows the Treasury to set recognition requirements by regulations. Recognition requirements are the requirements which must be satisfied by an exchange or clearing house in order both to become recognised, and to remain recognised.

520. *Subsection (2)* provides that if the regulations made under *subsection (1)* contain provisions relating to the default rules of a recognised body, then the Treasury has to have the approval of the Secretary of State before making the regulations. (The Secretary of State is responsible for insolvency matters.)

521. *Subsection (3)* defines default rules. These are rules which provide for action to be taken to settle market contracts in the event of a default; for example, the rules may specify the means for establishing the price at which a bargain should be made. These are necessary to protect against systemic risk in the financial markets. If contracts could

not be closed out in an orderly and speedy manner, a default by one market participant could spread quickly to large numbers of market participants.

522. *Subsection (4)* defines market contract by reference to Part VII of the Companies Act 1989 (or the corresponding Order in Northern Ireland). Market contracts in this context are those entered into by the exchange or clearing house or by the members of an exchange.

Section 287: Application by an investment exchange

523. This section allows an organisation to apply for recognition as a recognised investment exchange and sets out the information that the applicant must send to the Authority.

Section 288: Application by a clearing house

524. This section allows an organisation to apply for recognition as a clearing house and sets out the information that the applicant must send to the Authority.

Section 289: Applications: supplementary

525 This section allows the Authority to seek additional information, in whatever form it requires, in respect of any application for recognition under sections 287 and 288. It also allows the Authority to require verification of that information.

Section 290: Recognition orders

526. This section allows the Authority to make a recognition order if it is satisfied that the applicant meets the recognition requirements. The Authority is not obliged to make a recognition order in this circumstance and *subsection (3)* allows the Authority to take any information into account, and not just information concerning the recognition requirements, when deciding whether to grant recognition.

527. *Subsection (2)* requires the Treasury to give their approval under section 307 before the making of a recognition order. The role of the Treasury under that section concerns cases where there is an issue as to whether the rules and other regulatory provisions of the exchange or clearing house have a significantly adverse, and unjustified, effect on competition.

Section 291: Liability in relation to recognised body's regulatory functions

528. This section gives recognised investment exchanges immunity against legal action for damages in respect of anything done or omitted in the discharge of the recognised body's regulatory functions. This immunity does not apply where the act or omission was in bad faith or where it was unlawful as a result of section 6(1) of the Human Rights Act 1998. Under section 6(1) of that Act, it is unlawful for a public authority to act in a way which is incompatible with a right conferred by the European Convention on Human Rights and Fundamental Freedoms which is included in Schedule 1 to the 1998 Act.

Section 292: Overseas investment exchanges and overseas clearing houses

529. This section modifies the application procedures and requirements where the applicant concerned is an overseas investment exchange or clearing house.

530. In order to be recognised, an overseas applicant need not comply with the recognition requirements made by the Treasury under section 286. Instead, *subsection (2)* provides that the Authority may make a recognition order in respect of an overseas applicant if the requirements set out in *subsection (3)* are met. These requirements are that investors are afforded protection equivalent to that which they would have had if the overseas body were required to comply with the recognition requirements; that there are adequate default procedures; that the applicant is able and willing to co-operate with

the Authority; and that adequate arrangements are in place enabling the Authority to cooperate, for example through the sharing of information, with the overseas body's home State supervisor.

531. *Subsection (5)* makes some changes as to how other provisions of this Part work in respect of overseas bodies given that the relevant requirements which they have to meet are those set out in *subsection (3)* rather than the recognition requirements made by the Treasury.

Section 293: Notification requirements

532. *Subsections (1) to (4)* allow the Authority to make rules requiring a recognised body to give it notice of, and information about, specified events or information about the recognised body which the Authority reasonably requires to carry out its functions. The Authority can also specify when, and in what form, the information should be provided.

533. *Subsections (5) to (7)* place a duty on the recognised body to give the Authority immediate notice of new rules and guidance, or of changes to existing rules and guidance. Recognised bodies are also required to notify the Authority of changes to their clearing arrangements. S*ubsection (8)* provides that these duties do not apply to recognised overseas bodies. They are placed under different obligations under section 295.

Section 294: Modification or waiver of rules

534. This section gives the Authority power to waive or modify the notification rules it can make under sections 293 and 295, at the request of the recognised body or with their consent. *Subsection (4)* sets out the circumstances in which the Authority may do this.

Section 295: Notification: overseas investment exchanges and overseas clearing houses

535. This section requires overseas investment exchanges and clearing houses to produce a report at least once a year giving details of any events which have occurred over the year which may have an effect on competition, or which might affect the Authority's assessment of whether the requirements set out in section 292 are satisfied. The Authority can also make rules requiring that additional information should be included in the report.

Section 296: Authority's power to give directions

536. This section allows the Authority to direct a recognised body which has failed to satisfy the recognition criteria, or has failed to comply with other obligations under the Act (for example those in this Part) to take steps to remedy that failure. This power enables the Authority to deal with problems which are not sufficiently serious to merit withdrawal of recognition from the body concerned.

Section 297: Revoking recognition

537. This section allows the Authority to revoke the recognition of a body which no longer wishes to remain recognised, or which no longer meets the recognition criteria or which has failed to comply with other obligations under the Act.

Section 298: Directions and revocation: procedure

538. This section sets out the procedure the Authority must follow when it proposes to give a direction or make a revocation order. This includes giving the recognised body, its members and third parties who might be affected the right to make written representations. *Subsection (7)* allows the Authority to give a direction without following these procedures if it considers that it is essential to do so.

Section 299: Complaints about recognised bodies

539. This section provides that the Authority must establish a procedure for the investigation of complaints against recognised bodies where the complaint is relevant to the question of whether the body should remain recognised or not.

Section 300: Extension of functions of Tribunal

540. This section gives the Treasury a power to extend, by order, the jurisdiction of the Financial Services and Markets Tribunal to certain disciplinary proceedings brought by a recognised UK exchange or clearing house. An order may be made in respect of one or more specified recognised exchanges or clearing houses or in respect of recognised exchanges or clearing houses generally.

541. *Subsections (1) and (4)* make clear that jurisdiction may only be extended to cases involving internal disciplinary proceedings taken against members of recognised investment exchanges or recognised clearing houses for breaches of the rules of the exchange or clearing house in cases of behaviour which amounts to market abuse. Since it may be necessary to modify the provisions of the Act relating to proceedings before the Tribunal to accommodate the particular circumstances of a recognised exchange or clearing house, *subsection (3)* enables the Treasury to make any modifications that are necessary.

542. *Subsection (2)* deals with the circumstances in which jurisdiction may be extended. *Subsection (2)(a)* enables jurisdiction to be extended where the Treasury are satisfied that it is necessary to do so in order to ensure consistency between decisions taken in exchange or clearing house disciplinary proceedings involving market abuse and Tribunal decisions in such cases (including Tribunal decisions relating to the relevant disciplinary proceedings of other recognised exchanges or clearing houses). *Subsection (2)(b)* would enable the Treasury to extend the role of the Tribunal to recognised exchange or clearing house disciplinary proceedings in cases of market abuse if it should it prove necessary to do so in the future in the light of the developing jurisprudence of the European Court of Human Rights.

Section 301: Supervision of certain contracts

543. This section allows the Treasury, acting jointly with the Secretary of State, to make regulations which extend the provisions of Part VII of the Companies Act 1989 (or the equivalent provision of the Northern Ireland Order), with any appropriate modifications, to certain non-investment contracts. Part VII of the Companies Act 1989 disapplies various provisions of insolvency law for market contracts in order to protect against systemic risk in the financial markets.

544. *Subsection (2) and (3)* set out what kind of contracts can be covered by these regulations. There are two criteria:

- first, the contracts must be settled by someone who is on a list maintained by the Authority for the purposes of this section. The Treasury, under *subsection (4)*, has to approve the conditions set by the Authority for admission to this list and the arrangements for admission to and removal from the list;
- second, the Treasury and the Secretary of State have to be satisfied that it is appropriate for the Authority to supervise the settlement arrangements for these non-investment contracts. In coming to a view, the Treasury and Secretary of State must have regard to the extent to which the contracts are dealt in by persons supervised by the Authority.

545. *Subsection (10)* allows the Treasury and the Secretary of State, in making regulations under this section, to apply any of the provisions of this Act to the person settling these contracts. Without this power it would not be possible for the Authority to regulate such

persons on a statutory basis, since they would be clearing non-investment contracts and so would not require authorisation or exemption.

Chapter II: Competition Scrutiny

Section 302: Interpretation

546. This section describes the "regulatory provisions" (that is the rules, guidance, arrangements and particulars) and "practices" which are to be scrutinised under this Part to assess whether they have, or are intended or likely to have, a significantly adverse effect on competition as defined in this section.

Section 303: Initial report by Director

547. This section requires the Authority to send to the DGFT and to the Treasury all the regulatory provisions and any other relevant information received in support of an application for recognition. The DGFT must then issue a report as to whether any of these provisions has a significantly adverse effect on competition.

Section 304: Further reports by Director

548. This section requires the DGFT to keep all recognised investment exchanges and clearing houses under continuing competition scrutiny. If, at any time, the DGFT forms the view that any regulatory provision or practice has a significantly adverse effect on competition then he must make a report.

549. *Subsection (3)* provides that if the DGFT concludes that regulatory provisions or practices do not have such an effect then he has discretion as to whether to make a report.

Section 305: Investigations by Director

550. This section confers powers on the DGFT to enable him to carry out his functions under sections 303 and 304. The DGFT will be able to request relevant documents from any person, and to request relevant information from any business.

551. *Subsections (5) and (6)* provide that if a person fails to produce the information or documents required, then the DGFT may report the matter to the court. If the court is satisfied that there was no reasonable excuse for this failure, the person may be dealt with as if he were in contempt of court.

Section 306: Consideration by Competition Commission

552. This section concerns the role and duties of the Commission following receipt of a report from the Director General. Its functions and duties are in line with those set out in the analogous provisions in section 162 in Part X. This section is supplemented by the provisions of Schedule 14. (This Schedule also applies to section 162, which relates to the Commission's role in competition scrutiny of the regulating provisions and practices of the Authority.)

Section 307: Recognition orders: role of the Treasury

553. This section sets out the Treasury's powers to take action following an adverse report from the Commission on an application for a recognition order.

554. If the Commission's report concludes that no significantly adverse effect on competition exists, or such an effect does exist, but is justified, *subsection (2)* requires that the Treasury must approve the making of the recognition order unless exceptional circumstances exist to justify their refusal. If, however, the Commission's report is that a significantly adverse effect on competition exists, and is not justified, then *subsection (4)* requires that the Treasury, unless exceptional circumstances exist, should refuse to approve the making of the recognition order.

Section 308: Directions by the Treasury

555. This section concerns the Treasury's powers to take action following an adverse report from the Commission, other than a report on an application for a recognition order.

556. If the Commission's report is that the anti-competitive effect is not justified, *subsection (2)* requires that the Treasury give a "remedial direction". (A remedial direction is defined in *subsection (8)* as a direction to the Authority to either revoke the recognition of the body concerned, or to direct the body to take specified steps as set out in the direction.) However, *subsection (3)* provides that the Treasury need not give a direction either where the Treasury consider that it is not necessary as a result of action which has already been taken by the body concerned or by the Authority, or because exceptional circumstances exist which makes it inappropriate or unnecessary to give a direction. Conversely, if the Commission's conclusion is that the anti-competitive effect is justified, under *subsections (5) and (6)* the Treasury may nonetheless give a direction to the Authority to take action which the Treasury consider necessary because of exceptional circumstances of the case.

Section 309: Statements by the Treasury

557. This section makes provision for statements to be made by the Treasury when they decline to give a remedial direction under the preceding section.

558. *Subsection (1)* provides that if the Treasury decide not to give a remedial direction action following a Commission report that they should, they must produce a statement giving their reasons. *Subsection (2)* provides that if they do give such direction they must give details of this. In addition, if they have made a direction in a case where the Commission has concluded that the adverse effect on competition is justified, they must publish a statement giving their reasons for doing so.

Chapter III: Exclusion from the Competition Act 1998

Section 311: The Chapter I prohibition

559. This section makes clear that the prohibition of agreements preventing, restricting or distorting competition within the United Kingdom in Chapter I of the Competition Act 1998 does not apply to the constitution of a recognised investment exchange or clearing house or to a body which has applied for recognition; nor to the regulatory provisions of a recognised body; nor to a decision or practice of a recognised body, in respect of its regulatory functions; nor to an agreement the parties to which include a recognised body or person subject to its rules to the extent that the agreement is required or encouraged by the recognised body's regulatory provisions or practices.

Section 312: The Chapter II prohibition

560. This section makes clear that the prohibition of abuse of a dominant position in a market which may affect trade in the United Kingdom in Chapter II of the Competition Act 1998, does not apply to the regulatory provisions or practices of a recognised investment exchange or clearing house, nor to agreements entered into by its members, to the extent that these are required by the body's regulatory provisions.

Part Xix: Lloyd's

561. This Part of the Act makes a number of provisions which supplement other parts of the Act to bring the Society of Lloyd's ("the Society") within the general regulatory framework. These provisions are needed to reflect the unique legal status of the Society and its members, and the functions of the Council of Lloyd's ("the Council"), the governing body of the Society, under the Lloyd's Acts 1871-1982, in relation to the Lloyd's community.

562. Lloyd's is regulated for solvency purposes by the Authority in accordance with the arrangements under Part IV of the ICA 1982. The FS Act 1986 provides an exemption for Lloyd's and underwriting agents as respects investment business carried on by them in connection with or for the purposes of insurance business at Lloyd's. For most purposes, regulation of the Society has been undertaken by the Council. The Act gives the Authority considerable discretion as to how it discharges its obligations for the regulation of Lloyd's.

563. The external regulation of the Lloyd's community by the Authority is achieved by a number of different provisions in the Act. By virtue of this Part, the Society - a body corporate - is to be authorised to carry on certain regulated activities. The permission will be defined by the Authority, as if it had been granted under Part IV. Primarily, the permission will cover making arrangements which enable members to carry out contracts of insurance. The activities of managing and members' agents (or "underwriting agents") will become regulated activities for the purposes of the Act, and so underwriting agents will need have relevant permission under Part IV. As authorised persons, the Society and agents will be subject to the full range of the Authority's powers under the Act, including its rules and its powers of investigation and discipline and, ultimately, the power to withdraw authorisation, as is the case with other authorised persons under the general provisions of the Act.

564. Members of Lloyd's will benefit from an exemption from the need to be authorised in relation to contracts of insurance effected or carried out at Lloyd's. They will, nonetheless, be subject to regulatory arrangements as directed by the Authority under powers contained in this Part, and subject to the powers of the Council. As a minimum, the Authority will need to require the members to meet the solvency requirements laid down under the relevant EC directives. A member of Lloyd's would, however, need permission to carry on any other regulated activity, for example advising on investments.

Section 314: ***Authority's general duty***

565. It is not proposed that Lloyd's should be subject to full regulation by the Authority at the outset. Certain regulatory functions will be left with the Council. However, the Authority will at any time be able to take a greater degree of direct responsibility for regulation if it considers it appropriate and this section, therefore, places a duty on the Authority to keep matters under review.

Section 315: ***The Society: authorisation and permission***

566. This section makes the Society an authorised person, without it needing to submit an application. This is needed because, unlike most other current businesses, Lloyd's does not have an authorisation from an existing regulator that can be grandfathered.

567. *Subsection (3)* limits the activities for which the Society will have permission, at the time it becomes authorised, in broad terms to arranging deals in insurance contracts and syndicate participation, and for connected activities. The precise terms of the permission will depend on the activities specified for the purposes of section 22(1). *Subsection (4)* gives the Authority a power, where it considers it appropriate, to limit the scope of the permission, at the time the authorisation comes into force, or at any time thereafter. Lloyd's would apply for an extension of that permission in accordance with Part IV.

Section 316: ***Direction by Authority***

568. This section confers on the Authority power to give directions applying the general prohibition to members of Lloyd's or applying core provisions to members. This power can be used in relation to a member of Lloyd's, or members taken together, though they will not, at least at the outset, be authorised persons. Directions under this section may specify the extent to which the "core provisions" of the Act, as set out in section 317,

will apply to them and would impose requirements directly on the members which the Authority will be able monitor and enforce. The Authority could, for example, apply to members general rules requiring persons carrying out contracts of insurance to appoint an actuary to assess the extent of their liabilities. It could also require members to be authorised if it considers that appropriate.

*Section 317: **The core provisions***

569. The core provisions which the Authority may decide to apply to members of Lloyd's under section 316 relate to:

- the performance of regulated activities;
- rules and guidance;
- information gathering and investigations;
- control over authorised persons;
- compensation scheme;
- ombudsman scheme;
- auditors and actuaries;
- insolvency
- restitution and injunctions
- notices.

570. *Subsection (3)* enables the Authority to apply a core provision with modifications. This will enable the practical role played by the Society and underwriting agents in the day to day business affairs of members to be reflected in the regulatory arrangements.

*Section 318: **Exercise of powers through the Council***

571. This section gives the Authority an alternative mechanism to its power of direction under section 316. Instead of, or in addition to, giving a direction to the members of Lloyd's, the Authority can direct the Society or the Council to use their powers - such as the byelaw making powers of the Council under Lloyd's Act 1982 - to impose obligations on members. It would, therefore, be open to the Authority to set solvency requirements for Lloyd's members, perhaps specifying in a direction only the high level requirements required by the EC directives; the Council would then make byelaws specifying the detailed arrangements in accordance with the requirements of the direction. The Council would be responsible for enforcing its byelaws and for demonstrating to the Authority that the relevant requirements had been met. When exercising this power, the Authority may additionally impose requirements on the Council or the Society.

572. *Subsection (5)* also allows the Authority to use this power to direct the Council in respect of managing and members' agents, rather than exercising powers against them directly as authorised persons.

573. *Subsection (6)(a)* makes it clear that if the Authority chooses to give directions in this way, it is not precluded from using its other regulatory powers under the Act.

*Section 319: **Consultation***

574. This section sets out the procedure for giving a direction under sections 316 or 318. The procedures are similar to those that apply to other rule making functions.

*Section 320: **Former underwriting members***

575. This section disapplies the general prohibition from former members of Lloyd's in relation to contracts of insurance effected by them while they were members of the society. It gives the Authority powers to impose requirements on former members of Lloyd's, including members who decide to leave in the future, in relation to the insurance business carried on by them while they were members of Lloyd's until all their insurance liabilities have been discharged. A former member of Lloyd's would need to obtain permission from, and be authorised by, the Authority in order to carry on any other regulated activities under the Act.

*Section 321: **Requirements imposed under 320***

576. This section requires the Authority to follow the specified procedures when exercising the powers set out in section 320. The arrangements are consistent with other notice arrangements under the Act and they give former names on whom requirements are imposed the opportunity to make representations. *Subsection (11)* confers a right on former names to refer a matter to the Tribunal in certain circumstances.

*Section 322: **Rules applicable to former underwriting members***

577. This section, like section 320, confers on the Authority powers to impose requirements on former member of Lloyd's. Whereas section 320 would enable the Authority to impose specific requirements on former members, in much the same way as it would impose restrictions on a Part IV permission in relation to an authorised person, this section allows the Authority to make rules that will apply more generally to former members or classes of former member. The grounds for exercising the power are that the Authority considers it appropriate for the purpose of protecting policyholders. The procedures under section 319, including for example the consultation arrangements, apply to the exercise of this power.

*Section 323: **Transfer schemes***

578. This section confers on the Treasury a power to apply Part VII to transfers of business consisting of contracts of insurance from members of Lloyd's. This will ensure that appropriate regulatory scrutiny can be given to any proposed business transfers, and that any persons affected by the proposed transfer have the opportunity to make representations to the court.

Part Xx: Provision of Financial Services by Members of the Professions

579. This Part makes arrangements whereby professionals (such as solicitors, actuaries and accountants) who:

- are not carrying on mainstream regulated activities but
- are members of designated professional bodies,

will be exempt from the requirement to obtain permission from the Authority in order to carry out certain regulated activities. Additional tests are set out in section 327 which must be met in order for the professional to qualify for the exemption.

580. The arrangements under this Part include the safeguard of arms-length oversight by the Authority of the way in which the professional bodies supervise and regulate exempt professionals, and the way in which such professionals carry on regulated activities. This will involve, amongst other things, the Authority monitoring the effectiveness of the complaints and redress arrangements of designated professional bodies.

581. In addition, the Authority will be able to ban members of the professions who benefit from the exemption from carrying on regulated activities, where the circumstances

justify this. The Authority can also direct that the exemption be cut back on a more general class basis (so that, for example, certain categories of professional, carrying on certain types of activities, will no longer benefit from the exemption).

582. The Authority is also empowered to make rules requiring exempt professionals to disclose to their clients the fact that they are not regulated by the Authority.

*Section 325: **Authority's general duty***

583. This section obliges the Authority to keep itself informed about the way in which designated professional bodies supervise and regulate the carrying on of regulated activities by their members. It also requires the professional bodies to cooperate with the Authority so as to enable the Authority to fulfil its duty of arms-length oversight.

*Section 326: **Designation of professional bodies***

584. This section gives the Treasury the power to designate bodies for the purpose of section 325. Bodies will only be designated where they actively regulate the provision of financial services by their members.

*Section 327: **Exemption from the general prohibition***

585. This section sets out the tests which need to be met in order for a professional to qualify for the exemption, including:

- the professional must be a member of a professional body which is designated by the Treasury;
- the professional must not receive a commission from a third party in respect of the regulated activities unless he accounts to his client for it;
- the regulated activities must be provided in a way that is incidental and complementary to the provision of professional (for example, legal, actuarial or accountancy) services;
- the regulated activities must not relate to sensitive products (for example, life insurance). What amounts to a "sensitive product" is to be specified by the Treasury in regulations.

*Section 328: **Directions in relation to the general prohibition***

586. This section allows the Authority to direct that the exemption from the general prohibition is not to apply to certain classes of professional. The Authority may exercise this power, however, only where it is satisfied that it is desirable to do so in the interests of clients. A non-exhaustive list of factors to which the Authority must have regard in reaching that judgement is set out in the section.

*Section 329: **Orders in relation to the general prohibition***

587. This section enables the Authority to make an order which would have the effect of banning specified persons who are not fit and proper to carry on regulated activities. This is consistent with the arrangements for prohibition orders in relation to individuals under section 56.

*Section 330: **Consultation***

588. This section sets out the procedure for consulting on a direction. The procedure is consistent with that applying to similar arrangements in other parts of the Act.

Section 331: *Procedure on making or varying orders under section 329*

589. This section sets out the procedure which will apply when the Authority makes an order under section 329. The warning and decision notice procedure applied throughout the Act must be followed, and the person who is subject to an order can refer matters to the Tribunal.

Section 332: *Rules in relation to persons to whom the general prohibition does not apply*

590. This section allows the Authority to make rules requiring professionals carrying on exempt regulated activities to disclose to their clients that they are not authorised. It also requires the professional bodies to make rules designed to ensure that those members who benefit from the exemption will not carry on regulated activities which are not complementary to the provision of particular professional services to a particular client, although this does not extend to regulated activities conducted by professional firms as exempt persons under the Act. In order to be effective, those rules must be approved by the Authority.

Section 333: *False claims to be a person to whom the general prohibition does not apply*

591. This section makes it an offence for a person to describe himself (in whatever terms) as a person who has the benefit of the Part XX exemption in relation to a particular regulated activity, or behaves or otherwise holds himself out, in a manner which indicates (or which is reasonably likely to be understood as indicating) that he is such a person, when he is not.

592. *Subsection (2)* provides that in proceedings for an offence under this section it is a defence for the accused to show that he took all reasonable precautions and exercised all due diligence to avoid committing the offence.

593. Under*subsection (3)*, a person found guilty of this offence is liable on conviction to a maximum of 6 months imprisonment and a fine not exceeding level 5 on the standard scale (currently £5,000). If the offence results from the public display of material, *subsection (4)* a fine of level 5 is to multiplied by the number of days for which any material giving rise to the offence was on public display.

Part Xxi: Mutual Societies

594. This Part gives the Treasury powers by order to transfer the functions of the Building Societies Commission, the Friendly Societies Commission and the Chief Registrar of Friendly Societies and functions under the Industrial and Provident Societies Acts and the Credit Unions Act 1979. These transfers will be achieved by orders made under sections 334 to 339.

595. It is envisaged that the powers will be exercised to ensure that the functions which relate to the registration and regulation of societies under the existing legislation will be transferred to the Authority. For example, the functions to be transferred to the Authority are likely to include the power to require, or approve, a transfer of the business of a mutual society to another society or to a company.

596. The relevant legislation also confers power on the Building Societies Commission, Friendly Societies Commission and the Chief Registrar, often subject to the consent of the Treasury, to set requirements as to the registration and constitution of such societies. Such powers are exercised by statutory instrument. Those powers are different in character from the financial regulatory powers of the Authority under the Act. It is proposed that such functions will transfer to the Treasury.

597. These transfer provisions also include power for the Treasury to dissolve the existing bodies, it being envisaged that all their functions will have been transferred. The

Treasury will be able to make supplemental provision, for example, to transfer the property, rights and liabilities of bodies which are being dissolved or to amend the existing legislation in the light of the transfer of functions. For example, where the existing legislation divides functions as between the different parts of the United Kingdom, some consolidation may be required to reflect the fact that the Authority is a single corporate entity.

598. Schedule 18 makes certain amendments to the legislation governing mutuals. Further amendments to that legislation which are consequential on the provisions of this Act will be made by order under section 426.

Part Xxii: Auditors and Actuaries

599. This Part concerns the appointment, on a continuing, periodic or ad hoc basis, of auditors and actuaries by authorised persons. It imposes certain requirements, including a duty to disclose to the Authority information relevant to its functions under the Act. These provisions carry forward a number of similar provisions in existing legislation.

600. There are some similarities between the roles of auditors and actuaries, and they are therefore dealt with together in this part of the Act. However, there are also important differences, and these sections will give the Authority the power to act in ways which will recognise the difference in the detailed roles and responsibilities of the two professions.

601. Part XI of the Act gives the Authority various powers to gather information and investigate authorised persons, with section 166 in particular providing a power to require an authorised person to provide the Authority with a report by an accountant or other expert on a particular aspect of his business. Part XXII deals primarily with the duties and responsibilities of auditors and actuaries in respect of their work for authorised persons.

Section 340: Appointment

602. *Subsection (1)* gives the Authority the power to make rules to require authorised persons to appoint an auditor or actuary, where they are not already under a statutory obligation to do so (for example under Companies Act requirements). *Subsection (4)* allows the Authority to make rules concerning the terms, conditions, qualifications for, and notification of such appointments. The Authority will also be able to make an appointment itself if one is not made or if it has not received any notification.

603. *Subsection (2)* allows the Authority to make rules requiring any authorised person to produce periodic financial reports on its business, and to submit these for analysis and comment by an auditor or actuary.

604. *Subsection (5)* provides that an auditor or actuary appointed to act on a continuing basis or to produce a periodic report must comply with the relevant rules made by the Authority. These rules may also give the auditor or actuary such powers as the Authority judges necessary for them to carry out their duties.

Section 342: Information given by auditor or actuary to the Authority

605. This section concerns the duties and powers of auditors and actuaries of authorised persons to pass on information of regulatory importance to the Authority.

606. Auditors and actuaries of authorised persons will be members of professional bodies and will therefore be subject to rules made by their respective bodies as to how they treat confidential information. *Subsections (3) and (4)* ensure that auditors or actuaries who, in good faith, pass on information or express their opinion to the Authority will not be in breach of any duty of confidentiality to which they might otherwise be subject. This

protection applies whether or not the auditor or actuary acts in response to a request from the Authority.

607. *Subsections (5), (6) and (7)* give the Treasury a power to set out the circumstances in which auditors and actuaries must pass on information to the Authority. This information may relate to the affairs of either the authorised person concerned, or other persons. So far as auditors are concerned, the Treasury are required by EC directives to set out the circumstances in which such reports must be made, and it is intended to use this power to re-enact the rules necessary to comply with this requirement.

*Section 343: **Information given by auditor or actuary to the Authority: persons with close links***

608. This section concerns the duties and powers of auditors and actuaries to pass on information of regulatory significance to the Authority about persons having "close links" with authorised persons, including parent and subsidiary companies of an authorised person.

609. *Subsections (3) and (4)* ensure that auditors or actuaries of persons with close links to an authorised person, who, in good faith, pass on information or express their opinion to the Authority will not be in breach of any duty of confidentiality to which they might otherwise be subject. This protection applies whether or not the auditor or actuary acts in response to a request from the Authority.

610. *Subsections (5), (6) and (7)* give the Treasury a power under which they can make rules setting out the circumstances in which auditors and actuaries must pass on information to the Authority. This information may relate to the affairs of either the authorised person concerned, or other persons.

*Section 344: **Duty of auditor or actuary resigning etc. to give notice***

611. This section places a duty upon all auditors and actuaries of authorised persons appointed as a result of statute to notify the Authority of certain events, for example where they resign before the end of the period for which they were appointed. *Subsection (3)* also requires an auditor or actuary to pass on any facts connected with his ceasing to act for the authorised person which he thinks ought to be brought to the Authority's attention, or to make a positive statement to the Authority that he is not aware of any such facts.

*Section 345: **Disqualification***

612. Where the Authority believes that an auditor or actuary has failed to comply with any obligations under this Act, it may disqualify that auditor or actuary from acting for any particular authorised person, or class of authorised person. Any such disqualification may be lifted if the Authority is satisfied that the person concerned will in future comply with the obligations.

613. *Subsections (2) and (3)* require the Authority to serve a warning notice and decision notice, whilst *subsection (5)* confers a right to refer to the Tribunal any decision to disqualify.

*Section 346: **Provision of false or misleading information to auditor or actuary***

614. This section makes it a criminal offence for an authorised person, or an officer, controller or manager of an authorised person knowingly or recklessly to mislead an auditor or actuary appointed under the Act or as a result of provision contained in rules.

Part Xxiii: Public Record, Disclosure of Information and Co-Operation

615. This Part requires the Authority to compile and maintain a public record of authorised persons. It also imposes safeguards for the protection of confidential information.

616. The Authority, together with the competent authority for listing and the Secretary of State, will necessarily require access to confidential information. The Act provides them with powers to obtain this. It also contains safeguards to ensure that this information remains confidential, subject to allowing information to pass between them and other regulatory authorities where this is necessary for the performance of specific public functions (for example, to assist in the investigation and prosecution of crime). The passage of information between authorities is subject to conditions relating to the purpose of disclosure and, in some cases, the identity of the person to whom the information is disclosed. These conditions are often referred to as "gateways". This area is already subject to detailed constraints under EC law. The Act, together with the regulations to be made under the powers conferred by these provisions, will create a confidentiality regime very similar to those under the predecessor legislation. The creation of a single regulator will however allow some rationalisation of the existing structure.

Section 347: The record of authorised persons etc.

617. This section places an obligation on the Authority to maintain a record of certain details about authorised persons and other categories of persons set out in subsection (1). The record must include details of the services provided by authorised persons, the addresses of authorised persons and other categories of specified persons, and any other information the Authority thinks is appropriate. The record must be available for inspection by members of the public, at a place and at times determined by the Authority. The Authority must allow members of the public to obtain a copy of the record, or a part of it. The Authority may charge for providing such copies.

Section 348: Restrictions on disclosure of confidential information by Authority etc.

618. *Subsections (2), (3) and (4)* define what is, and what is not, to be regarded as confidential information. *Subsection (1)* makes clear that this information is not to be disclosed by a "primary recipient", or a person who has received the information from a primary recipient, without the consent of the person from whom it was obtained and, if different, the person to whom it relates. *Subsection (5)* lists primary recipients.

Section 349: Exceptions from section 348

619. This section makes clear that, notwithstanding the restrictions in section 348, confidential information may be disclosed if this is in accordance with regulations made by the Treasury. It also gives the Treasury the power to make such regulations where disclosure would facilitate the carrying out of a public function. This power will be used to create various "gateways" between the primary recipients and other organisations for various specified purposes.

Section 350: Disclosure of information by the Inland Revenue

620. This section creates a mechanism, or gateway, through which information held by the Inland Revenue, which would otherwise be subject to a legal obligation of confidentiality, may, in certain circumstances be passed to the Authority or to the Secretary of State. *Subsection (2)* makes clear that this disclosure may be made only by, or under the authority of, the Commissioners of Inland Revenue.

621. *Subsection (1)* provides that Revenue information may be disclosed under this section only for the purpose of assisting an investigator appointed by the Authority or the Secretary of State under section 168 in his task, or to assist the Authority or the Secretary of State in taking a decision whether or not to appoint such an investigator. Once information has been disclosed, *subsection (4)* provides that it may only be used for the purposes of taking a decision whether or not to appoint an investigator, or to further an investigation, if an investigator has been appointed, or in any criminal proceedings

or regulatory action, including proceedings before the Financial Services and Markets Tribunal, that may arise out of an investigation.

622. *Subsection (5)* provides that onward disclosure of information received under this section is prohibited, except in the case of proceedings before a court or the Tribunal arising out of an investigation, or if this is done with a view to the institution of such proceedings, or if it takes place with the consent or the authority of the Commissioners of Inland Revenue. *Subsection (6)* makes clear, however, that this does not prevent disclosure of information to a person to whom it could have been disclosed under *subsection (1)*.

*Section 350: **Competition information***

623. This section makes provision, together with Schedule 19, for the protection of information obtained by the DGFT and the Commission under their powers of competition scrutiny under the Act. It applies to information obtained under all of the various competition scrutiny provisions in the Act, that is to say the provisions covering the competent authority for listing in Part VI, the Authority in Part X, and the recognised investment exchanges and clearing houses in Part XVIII.

624. *Subsection (1)* provides that it is an offence improperly to disclose "competition information". "Competition information" is defined in *subsection (5)* as information about the affairs of a particular individual or body, which is not in the public domain, and which was obtained under powers in a competition provision of the Act.

625. *Subsection (2)* sets out the circumstances in which disclosure will not be regarded as improper, and which is therefore permissible. These circumstances basically fall into two classes. First, where the person to whom the information relates, and if different the person from whom it is obtained, have given their consent to disclosure. Second, when this would serve one of a number of defined public purposes. These purposes include the fulfilment of the UK's obligations under EC law, the investigation and prosecution of crime, civil proceedings under the competition provisions of the Act, and finally the disclosure of information to a number of bodies having various statutory functions, to assist them in carrying out these functions. The bodies and the statutes concerned are listed in Schedule 19.

*Section 352: **Offences***

626. This section makes clear that unauthorised disclosure or use of confidential information is a criminal offence, subject to the defences provided for in *subsection (6),* and sets out the penalties for these offences. These provisions reproduce the existing offences in this area.

*Section 353: **Removal of other restrictions on disclosure***

627. This section enables the Treasury to make regulations permitting disclosure of information held by third parties to the Authority to assist it in carrying out its functions. It also enables regulations to be made to allow the disclosure of information by various other entities carrying out functions under this Act, for example the compensation scheme manager, in order to assist with these functions. The purpose of this section is to enable the Treasury to create gateways, for example overriding confidentiality obligations to which the prescribed persons are subject, if it is appropriate that such persons should be able to disclose information either to the Authority or to third parties for the purposes of functions connected to the Act.

*Section 354: **Authority's duty to cooperate with others***

628. This section places a duty on the Authority to take such steps as it considers appropriate to co-operate and share information, which it is not otherwise prevented from disclosing by virtue of the provisions of this Part, with other bodies or persons, whether in the

United Kingdom or elsewhere, who have functions broadly equating to those of the Authority, or who have a role in relation to the prevention and detection of financial crime. It carries forward the provision in paragraph 5 of Schedule 7 of the FS Act 1986, which places a similar duty on the Authority.

Part Xxiv: Insolvency

629. Insolvency and winding up are relevant to regulation for two reasons. First, there are implications for existing customers if a financial service business becomes insolvent. Second, winding up may itself be part of the appropriate regulatory response to events. Thus it may be desirable to wind up a company to protect not just the interests of customers who have entered into contracts with it, but also those who might do business with it in future, if it continued to trade. Subject to the particular provisions of Part VII of the Companies Act 1989 for transactions carried out on regulated markets, the general law of insolvency applies, and will continue to apply, to most financial services businesses, as it does to other businesses. However, it is supplemented by provisions which allow the regulators, alongside creditors, to petition the court for the winding up of an authorised business on the grounds of insolvency, and, alongside the Secretary of State, to petition the court to wind up an authorised business on the grounds that this would be just and equitable.

630. Different arrangements apply to certain mutual societies. The arrangements under the relevant legislation, for example the Building Societies Act 1986, will continue to apply to relevant societies, with functions transferred in that case from the Building Societies Commission to the Authority in accordance with the provisions of Part XXI.

631. The insolvency provisions of the Act are intended to build upon these existing arrangements, establishing, so far as is practicable, a common approach across all sectors. Sections 356, 357, 367 and 375 provide the Authority with the power to ask the court to initiate various insolvency procedures. Sections 356, 362, 363, 365, 371 and 374 make clear that the Authority has the right to be heard by the court in insolvency proceedings instigated by third parties. Sections 369, 376, 377, 378 and 379 carry forward provisions of the ICA 1982 dealing with the insolvency of insurance companies (which because of the particular nature of insurance business, must in some respects be dealt with in a different way to other authorised persons).

632. At the same time, the Part will fill a number of gaps in the coverage of the predecessor regimes. Section 359 will allow the Authority to ask the court to make an administration order in respect of authorised businesses, as an alternative to winding up. Section 372 will give the Authority powers to petition the court to declare bankrupt an insolvent sole trader providing financial services. Sections 360 and 366 make changes to the insolvency regime for insurers.

633. Part XV (Financial Services Compensation Scheme) is also relevant to customers of authorised firms in financial difficulties.

Voluntary arrangements

*Section 356: **Authority's powers to participate in proceedings: company voluntary arrangements***

634. Insolvency legislation allows companies in financial difficulties to propose a voluntary arrangement with creditors; that is, for creditors to agree to take a proportion of what they were owed as a final settlement of their debts. If agreed, such an arrangement is binding on all creditors who were aware of the proposal, subject to their right to ask the court to intervene if the arrangement seems improper or unfair. This section gives the Authority the right to apply to the court in the same way as a creditor, and also makes clear that the Authority may be represented in any such proceedings initiated by a creditor.

Section 357: Authority's powers to participate in proceedings: individual voluntary arrangements

635. In England and Wales and in Northern Ireland insolvency law provides that an individual who is in financial difficulties may apply to the court for a moratorium during which he may prepare a proposal to his creditors for settlement of his debts. Whilst this moratorium is in force the individual is protected against the presentation of a bankruptcy petition.

636. *Subsection (1)* of this section provides that the Authority is entitled to be heard by the court on an application for such a moratorium, if this is made by an individual who is an authorised person. *Subsections (3) and (4)* provide that the Authority is entitled to send a representative to attend and speak at any meeting of creditors summoned to consider a proposal which a debtor brings forward, and that it shall be informed of the results of any such meeting. *Subsection (5)* goes on to provide the Authority with the same rights as creditors to challenge in court a decision by the meeting to agree a creditor's proposal, or to challenge the implementation of an agreed proposal, if it believes that this is in some way unfair or irregular, whilst *subsection (6)* provides that the Authority is entitled to be heard by the court if any other person makes such a challenge.

Section 358: Authority's powers to participate in proceedings: trust deeds for creditors in Scotland

637. Section 357 provides the Authority with powers to be involved in individual voluntary arrangements proposed for authorised persons. Such arrangements are only possible in England, Wales and Northern Ireland. This section makes provision for the Authority to have certain rights in the equivalent arrangement in Scots law (a voluntary trust deed for creditors within the meaning of section 5(4A) of the Bankruptcy (Scotland) Act 1985).

638. The purpose of a trust deed under Scots law is to allow a person who cannot pay his debts to hand over his assets to a trustee, who may then arrange a settlement with his creditors as a alternative to proceedings for sequestration under the 1985 Act. *Subsections (1) and (2)* provide that where a trust deed is granted in respect of an authorised person, the trustee must, as soon as he becomes aware that the person concerned is an authorised person, inform the Authority, and send it copies of the deed and any other documents which he has sent to the creditors.

639. Under *subsection (3)* the Authority is given the same rights as certain creditors who have not received notice of the trust deed, or who have objected to it, to petition for the sequestration of a debtor who is an authorised person.

640. If the trustee proposes at any stage to hold a meeting of creditors, *subsections (4) and (5)* require him to inform the Authority, which will have the right to send a representative to attend and speak at the meeting. However, the Authority will not have the right to vote at the meeting, except on those occasions where it is itself a creditor of the person concerned.

Administration orders

Section 359: Petitions

641. General insolvency law provides for the court to place a company or partnership into administration, that is to allow it to continue in business, under the supervision of an administrator, as an alternative to winding it up. This section allows the Authority to ask the court to do this in respect of present or former financial services businesses and appointed representatives or persons who are or have carried on financial services business without authorisation, where it would be in consumers' interests for the business to remain in being, rather than be wound up. It also provides that for such

persons failure to pay money due to consumers on time shall count as sufficient evidence to allow the initiation of administration proceedings.

Section 360: Insurers

642. At present, the law prohibits insurance companies from being put into administration. When insolvency law first made provisions for administration in 1985, it was not clear whether this procedure would be appropriate for such companies, given the special nature of insurance business. Experience has shown that it may be helpful to make this option available, so this section gives the Treasury the power to make an order removing the prohibition in relation to insurers. "Insurers" for these purposes will be defined in regulations made by the Treasury.

Section 362: Authority's powers to participate in proceedings

643. This section makes clear that when a creditor or other third party asks the court to place in administration a person who is doing or has done financial services business, or who is or has been an appointed representative, or persons who are or have carried on financial services business without authorisation, then the Authority shall have the right to be represented at the hearing. It also gives the Authority the right to receive any information or proposals sent by the administrator to creditors, to attend and speak at any meeting of creditors called to discuss the administration, and to have the same rights as creditors to ask the court to intervene, if it considers that the administration is being carried out improperly or unfairly. It also gives the Authority the same power that creditors have under section 425 of the Companies Act (and the equivalent Northern Ireland provision), where a scheme is proposed to settle some or all of the debts of a company in administration, to ask the court that this be put to a vote of creditors.

Receivership

Section 363: Authority's powers to participate in proceedings

644. This section provides that when a receiver is appointed in respect of a company which is or was an authorised person, or an appointed representative, or which is or has been carrying on regulated activities without authorisation, the Authority is entitled to be represented at any hearing at which the receiver applies to the court for directions. It also provides that the Authority has the right to receive any information or proposals sent by the receiver to creditors and to attend and speak at any meeting of creditors called to discuss the winding up.

Voluntary winding up

Section 365: Authority's powers to participate in proceedings

645. This section gives the Authority the right to be represented at any court proceedings to wind up voluntarily a financial services company, other than an long term insurer. It also provides the Authority with the same powers that creditors have to ask the court to decide any questions arising out of the winding up, or to order that a scheme, under section 425 of the Companies Act (or the equivalent Northern Ireland provision), to settle some or all of the debts of the company, should be put to a vote of creditors. In addition, it gives the Authority the right to receive any notice or document required to be sent to creditors and to attend and speak at any creditors' meeting.

Section 366: Insurers carrying on long-term business

646. Under the predecessor legislation, there is a prohibition on the voluntary winding up of insurance companies carrying on long term, or life assurance, business. The reason is that if such companies went into voluntary liquidation the rights of endowment policyholders would accrue, so that they would be entitled only to the current value of

their policy, and not to the terminal bonuses they would expect if their policies ran on to the end of their term. This section removes this absolute prohibition, but provides that voluntary winding up can only take place with the Authority's prior permission. This will allow the Authority to ensure that winding up will only proceed subject to arrangements being made to meet the legitimate expectations of policyholders.

Winding up by the court

Section 367: Winding-up petitions

647. This section provides that the Authority may ask the court compulsorily to wind up any company or partnership which is doing or has done financial services business or which is or has carried on financial services business without authorisation. The powers also apply to an appointed representative. As with the other provisions in this part which empower the Authority to initiate proceedings, this enables the Authority to act on behalf of consumers, who could in theory take action themselves, but may in practice lack the resources and expertise to do so. The court may agree to this in cases where the business cannot pay its debts, or where it decides that it would be "just and equitable" to wind up the business. The Authority might make an application under the latter ground if, for example, a business had been guilty of such serious rule breaches that the Authority had found it necessary to cancel its permission in order to protect the public. This section also provides that for such businesses failure to pay money due to consumers on time can count as sufficient evidence to allow the initiation of insolvency proceedings.

Section 368: Winding-up petitions: EEA and Treaty firms

648. This section makes clear that the Authority can only petition under section 367 for the winding up of a business which is authorised in another EEA State, and is entitled to provide financial services in the United Kingdom because of that authorisation, when it has been asked to do so by the home State regulator concerned. This is because the issues that generally arise in relation to the winding up of a business are issues which are primarily the concern of the home State regulator, rather than of the host State where the business is being carried on.

Section 371: Authority's powers to participate in proceedings

649. This section makes clear that when a creditor, or other third party, asks the court to wind up a person who is doing or has done financial services business, or who is or has been an appointed representative, the Authority has the right to be represented at the hearing, and at any subsequent hearing. It also provides that the Authority has the right to receive any information or proposals sent by the liquidator to creditors and to attend and speak at any meeting of creditors called to discuss the winding up, and to have the same rights as creditors to ask the court to intervene. It also gives the Authority the same power that creditors have under section 425 of the Companies Act (or the equivalent Northern Ireland provision), where a scheme is proposed to settle some or all of the debts of a company being wound up, to ask the court that this be put to a vote of creditors.

Bankruptcy

Section 372: Petitions

650. Section 367 gives the Authority power to ask the courts to wind up companies or partnerships doing financial services business. The section also confers a power in respect of sole traders doing financial services business. The Authority will be able to petition for the bankruptcy of such persons, or in Scotland, for the sequestration of their estate, if they are or appear unable to pay their debts to consumers. It should be noted, however, that here, as in insolvency law generally, inability to pay debts is the only ground on which a sole trader can be made bankrupt - there is no equivalent to the

provision covering companies and partnerships that these may be wound up because the court feels it is "just and equitable" to do so. This is because sole traders' business affairs are not legally distinct from their personal finances.

Section 374: Authority's powers to participate in proceedings

651. This section makes clear that when a creditor, or other third party, asks the court to make a bankruptcy order for, or in Scotland to sequestrate the estate of, an individual who is doing or has done financial services business, then the Authority shall have the right to be represented at the hearing, and at any subsequent hearing. It also provides that the Authority has the right to receive any report sent by an insolvency practitioner to creditors and to attend and speak at any meeting of creditors called to discuss the bankruptcy.

Provisions against debt avoidance

Section 375: Authority's right to apply for an order

652. The Insolvency Act 1986 provides creditors, liquidators and administrators of insolvent persons with the right to ask the court to set aside transactions which appear to have been entered into to defraud creditors (that is, where assets are transferred as a gift, or sold at less than their full value, with the intention of putting them beyond the reach of creditors). This section provides the Authority with an equivalent right to make an application to the court in relation to transactions entered into in the course of financial services business.

Supplemental provisions concerning insurers

Section 376: Continuation of contracts of long-term insurance where insurer in liquidation

653. This section provides for the business of an insolvent insurer so far as it relates to contracts of long-term insurance to be transferred to another company, rather than for the policyholders to receive a share of the assets available on winding up. Policyholders of long term insurers face different problems to most consumers if the company fails. They enter into agreements, for example for pensions, which are designed to last many years, and the benefits they expect to receive build up over time. Also, the terms of the contract (and importantly the premium) are set at the outset. If, for example, during the course of the contract they were to develop an illness they might not then be able to obtain alternative cover. For these reasons, it is desirable, where possible, to maintain the insurer's business as a going concern, or to find an alternative insurer to take over its policies, rather than allowing it to be wound up.

Section 377: Reducing the value of contracts instead of winding up

654. This section is intended to facilitate timely payments on, or the transfer of, insurance contracts of a company which has become insolvent, rather than leaving these to be matters to be resolved at the end of an insolvency process, which may take a considerable period of time.

Section 378: Treatment of assets on winding up

655. This section empowers the Treasury to make regulations to allow for the separate treatment in insolvency situations of an insurer's contracts of long-term and general insurance, given the special characteristics of long term business (referred to in the note on section 376 above).

*Section 379: **Winding-up rules***

656. This section enables the making of rules to deal with the winding up of insurers, under the powers of the Insolvency Act 1986.

Part Xxv: Injunctions and Restitution

657. This Part is concerned with the Authority's (and in certain cases the Secretary of State's) power to seek injunctions and restitution orders from the High Court, or in Scotland the Court of Session, against both authorised and unauthorised persons where it appears that certain requirements have been, or might be, contravened. Section 384 also gives the Authority the power to require restitution to be paid without having to apply to the courts for a restitution order, but this direct power can only be used against authorised persons.

658. The powers contained in this Part may be exercised by the Authority in relation to breaches which constitute an offence under the Act, or which the Authority has power to prosecute under section 402, or any breach of any other requirement imposed by or under the Act, such as a rule made under Part X. The Secretary of State may exercise the powers in relation to any breach which constitutes an offence which the Act gives him the power to prosecute under section 401.

*Section 380: **Injunctions***

659. This section sets out the powers of the court to make injunctive orders on the application of the Authority or Secretary of State and the grounds on which they may exercise those powers. The court may make three types of order: an order restraining the contravention of certain requirements (*subsection (1)*), an order directing remedial action to be taken when there has been such a contravention (*subsection (2)*) and an order freezing the assets of someone who has contravened certain requirements or been knowingly involved in a contravention (*subsection (3)*).

660. The first of these is a preventative measure. Under*subsection (1)(a)* an order can be made restraining a person from contravening a requirement where the court believes they are reasonably likely to do so. Where a contravention has already occurred, under *subsection (1)(b)* the courts can restrain a person from doing so again.

661. Where there are clear steps that can be taken either by the person who has contravened a requirement or by a person knowingly concerned in the contravention, under *subsection (2)* the court may order a person to take those steps. This is a corrective power. For example, an order may simply require a person to meet commitments they have entered into but so far failed to discharge. *Subsection (5)* provides that the remedial action that the court may order under *subsection (2)* may include orders to mitigate the impact of a contravention even if it is not, strictly speaking, possible to remedy it. For example where a person has published a misleading advertisement, the Authority could apply to the court for an order requiring the person to publish a correction. This would not be of use to anyone who had taken action on the basis of the original advertisement but would prevent others doing so in the future.

662. An order made under*subsection (3)* to freeze a person's assets is similar to a Mareva injunction[1] apart from its timing: a Mareva injunction may only be applied for where court proceedings have been commenced or are imminent whereas this section gives the Authority or Secretary of State an independent power to apply to the court for an asset-freezing order on the grounds that they believe a breach may have occurred. The power does not prevent separate applications for Mareva injunctions.

663. *Subsection (6)* sets out the range of requirements the contravention or likely contravention of which may be grounds for an order under this section. These are

1 A Mareva injuction (now known as a 'freezing order') is a remedy a court may use to prevent assets being removed, charged or otherwise dealt with in a way that could prejudice a legal action that is otherwise being, or about to be, pursued.

requirements imposed by or under the Act, including the Authority's rules made under Part X, plus the various requirements a breach of which constitutes an offence under the Act, such as the general prohibition under Part II. In addition, the powers may be exercised for breaches of requirements imposed by other Acts which constitute offences which the Authority has power to prosecute. The Authority's power in that respect is set out in section 402.

Section 381: ***Injunctions in cases of market abuse***

664. This section provides the Authority with the power to apply to the court for injunctive orders in cases of market abuse. The Secretary of State has no powers under this section in relation to market abuse. The types of orders which the court may make are the same for cases of market abuse under this section as for contraventions of requirements under the previous section.

Section 382: ***Restitution orders***

665. This section gives the court the power, on the application of the Authority or the Secretary of State, to order restitution to be paid by a person who has contravened a requirement or been knowingly involved in a contravention. The court must be satisfied that the contravention has led either to the person ordered to pay restitution accruing profits or to others suffering loss or being adversely affected in other ways. It is possible for an application for a restitution order to be combined with an application for an injunction.

666. Under *subsection (2)*, the court has discretion to decide what is an appropriate sum for a person to have to pay taking into account the size of any profits which have accrued and the extent to which persons have suffered loss or been adversely affected. The restitution is initially paid to the Authority, but the Authority is then required to distribute the money among people chosen by the court. These must be those people who appear to the court to have been directly affected by the contravention, or to whom the profits may be attributed, for example because it was their funds that were used to make a particular investment which gave rise to the profits.

667. *Subsections (4)* and *(5)* give the court powers to require further information from potential recipients of restitution orders to assist the court in determining what profits have accrued to them, to what extent others have been affected by a contravention or how to distribute the money. The court may also require this information to be verified.

668. *Subsection (7)* provides that the fact that the Authority or the Secretary of State has made an application under this section for a restitution order does not prevent someone taking a private action for restitution in respect of the same matter. The court is likely to have regard to the question of whether any payments have already been made by a person in determining whether to order restitution in any particular case.

669. The range of requirements the contravention of which can give rise to an application to the courts under this section for a restitution order is the same as for injunctions under section 380. These are set out in *subsection (9)*.

Section 383: ***Restitution orders in cases of market abuse***

670. This section provides the Authority with the power to apply to the court for restitution orders against persons who it is satisfied have engaged in market abuse. The Secretary of State has no powers under this section. The provisions of this section are equivalent to those in the section above for restitution orders following the contravention of a requirement. Again, the court has discretion to determine the amount of restitution paid and the eventual recipients of that restitution who must be persons directly affected by the market abuse. The court also has similar powers as under section 382 to require further information from the person who has engaged in market abuse. However under this section the court may not make an order if it is satisfied that the person

concerned believed, on reasonable grounds, that market abuse was not involved, or took all reasonable precautions and exercised all due diligence to avoid market abuse. This restriction is analogous to the provisions of section 123(2) which apply where the Authority wishes to impose a penalty in relation to market abuse.

Section 384: ***Power of Authority to require restitution***

671. This section gives the Authority the direct power to require an authorised person to pay restitution, without having to go through the court, although the authorised person does have the right to refer the matter to the Tribunal under section 386. The Authority can order restitution to be paid by:

- authorised persons who have contravened a requirement under the Act or who have committed an offence mentioned in section 402;
- authorised persons who have been knowingly involved in such a contravention;
- any person, whether authorised or not, who has engaged in market abuse.

672. The Secretary of State has no direct powers under this Part to require restitution.

673. The grounds for the Authority using this power are set out in *subsections (1) and (2)*. These are that the Authority is satisfied that the person has done the misdeed and that, because of it, either profits have accrued to that person or one or more people have suffered loss or been adversely affected.

674. The Authority may require someone to pay restitution of an amount which it considers to be just, taking into account the profits that have accrued and/or the extent of the loss or adverse effect suffered. The money is to be paid to people who have been directly affected by the contravention or offence, or to whom profits are attributable, as under sections 382 and 383. Where restitution is sought via a court order, the money is paid initially to the Authority, but when the Authority uses its power under this section to require restitution directly, *subsection (5)* provides for the money to be paid straight to the final recipients. The Authority may determine the arrangements for payment.

Section 385: ***Warning notices***

675. This section requires the Authority to issue a warning notice informing someone of any proposal to require them to pay restitution under section 384. A warning notice must comply with the provisions of section 387. The warning notice must specify the amount of restitution proposed.

Section 386: ***Decision notices***

676. This section provides that if the Authority decides to require restitution to be paid, it must send a decision notice to the person in relation to whom this power is being exercised. The section also provides a right to refer the Authority's decision to the Tribunal.

Part Xxvi: Notices

677. Various provisions of the Act relate to the Authority taking decisions, for example as to whether to grant, or to withdraw, authorisations and approvals, or whether to take other regulatory action, such as imposing financial penalties or making public statements. The relevant provisions of the Act require the Authority in some cases to give warning and decision notices, and in others to give other kinds of notice This Part is concerned with the Authority's procedures during, before and after the process of serving these notices as well as the information which they are to include. In particular, the Part requires the Authority to act in accordance with a published set of procedures.

*Section 387: **Warning notices***

678. This section provides that a warning notice must be in writing and must set out the reasons for the proposed course of action. It must also state whether section 394 (Access to Authority material) applies.

679. *Subsection (2)* gives any person who receives a warning notice an opportunity to make representations to the Authority. The Authority may specify the period available for representations, provided it allows a minimum of 28 days from the date of the notice. The Authority must then decide whether to give the person a decision notice within a reasonable period.

*Section 388: **Decision notices***

680. A decision notice must be in writing and must set out the reasons for the course of action. It also requires the Authority to explain a right of access to Authority material under section 394 and rights to refer the case to the Tribunal (including the procedure for doing so).

681. If a decision notice follows a warning notice, the action proposed in it must be action the Authority has powers to take under the same Part of the Act. The Authority can issue a further decision notice altering the action proposed in an earlier notice, but only with the consent of the person concerned.

*Section 389: **Notices of discontinuance***

682. This section requires a "notice of discontinuance" to be issued when the Authority decides not to proceed with action proposed in a warning notice (section 387) or in relation to which a decision notice (section 388) was given.

683. However a notice of discontinuance does not have to be given if the effect is purely to grant an application made by the person in question. In such cases the Act generally contains express provision requiring written notice to be given of the grant of the application.

*Section 390: **Final notices***

684. This section requires a "final notice" to be issued to confirm and give effect to an action proposed in a decision notice (and to require payment in the case of a penalty) whenever the period for referring a matter to the Tribunal has expired, or if it has been referred, whenever the matter has been finally determined by the Tribunal or the higher courts. If the matter was referred to the Tribunal then the final notice will give effect to the directions of the Tribunal (or the higher courts if there has been a appeal).

685. *Subsection (7)* requires the final notice to set out details of the action which is being taken and the date when it is to be taken. Particular requirements for certain categories of case are given in *subsections (3) to (6)*. For example the notice must include the terms of any public statement which is to be made and details of the manner and date of publication, or the amount of any financial penalty and details of how and when it is to be paid. The period for making payments must not be less than 14 days beginning with the date on which the final notice is given, after which the Authority may recover any outstanding amount as a debt owed to it.

686. A similar 14 day minimum period must be allowed for making restitution as required under section 384, after which any outstanding obligations are enforceable through an application by the Authority to the courts (for an injunction in England and Wales and Northern Ireland or, in Scotland, for an order under section 45 of the Court of Session Act 1988).

*Section 391: **Publication***

687. This section establishes common rules on publication of decisions which:

- prevent the Authority from publishing details about warning and decision notices;
- enable the Authority to publish appropriate details of a discontinued decision, but only if the person to whom the notice is given consents; and
- require the Authority to publish appropriate information about a final notice, but omitting information which would be unfair to the person to whom the notice relates or prejudicial to the interests of consumers.

688. The provision for publishing details of a final notice applies equally to a supervisory notice (as defined in section 395) but only when such a notice takes effect. The procedure on giving a supervisory notice is set out under the description of section 53 above. If the notice so states, it may take effect immediately, or on a particular date. Otherwise it will take effect only once it is no longer "open to review". *Subsection (8)* of this section provides that a supervisory notice is "open to review" until after the period for referring the matter to the Tribunal has expired and until any reference or further appeal has been finally determined.

*Section 392: **Application of** sections 393 **and** 394*

689. Sections 393 and 394, described below, confer additional procedural rights relating to third parties and to disclosure of Authority material. However those rights apply only in cases, other than those involving the Authority responding to an application, which are governed by the warning notice and decision notice procedure. This section lists the particular sections of the Act where sections 393 and 394 apply.

*Section 393: **Third party rights***

690. Where this section applies (see section 392 above) it confers rights on any person (a "third party") who is identified in prejudicial terms in the reasons contained in a warning notice or decision notice. Third parties are given the right to receive a copy of the notice, and to make representations or refer the matter to the Tribunal in the same way as the person who is the subject of the Authority's proposed action. However *subsections (2) and (6)* provide that a third party does not need to be given a copy of a notice which identifies him if a separate warning or decision notice has been given to him in relation to the same matter, and *subsection (7)* provides a further exception where it is impracticable to contact the third party.

691. *Subsection (13)* provides that third party notices must describe the rights which third parties also have under section 394 below. *Subsections (5) and (14)* provide a third party with rights to receive copies of subsequent notices in relation to the same matter.

*Section 394: **Access to Authority material***

692. Where this section applies (see section 392 above), the Authority is required to give any person who is the subject of a warning or decision notice, or who has received a copy of such a notice as a third party, access to certain categories of material. *Subsection (1)(a)* requires access to be given to any material on which the Authority relied in taking the decision in question. *Subsection (1)(b)* requires access to be given to material which the Authority considers might undermine that decision.

693. The latter category does not apply to all material in the Authority's possession but only to material which the Authority considered in reaching its decision, or which it obtained in connection with, that is in investigation of, the matter in question (see the definition of "secondary material" in *subsection (6)*).

694. The right of access to Authority material is subject to the following exceptions. First, the Authority may refuse access to material relating to a different case which was taken into account only for the purposes of comparison with the case in question. Secondly, it may refuse access to "excluded material", defined as covering "protected items" as defined in section 413, and material intercepted under (or indicating the existence of) a warrant for the interception of communications. If access to material is refused on the grounds that it is subject to legal professional privilege, the Authority must give written notice to the person concerned.

695. Finally the Authority can refuse access to material which it would not be in the public interest to disclose (that is, material subject to public interest immunity) or to commercially sensitive material which it would not be fair to disclose. In these cases the Authority must notify the person and give its reasons for refusing.

Section 395: ***The Authority's procedures***

696. This section concerns the Authority's decision-making procedures. It is for the Authority to decide on its procedures but *subsection (2)* requires that, to avoid prejudice, they should be designed to ensure that the task of deciding whether to issue a warning, decision or supervisory notice and the task of collecting relevant information should be carried out by different people. However, *subsections (3) and (4)* provide that the procedures can provide for this requirement to be waived for supervisory notices (as defined in *subsection (13)*) if necessary to protect the interests of consumers, so long as the decision is taken by a person at an appropriate level of seniority given the importance of the decision.

697. The Authority is required by *subsections (5) and (6)* to issue and publish a statement describing its procedures. It must be published in a way appearing to the Authority best calculated to bring it to the attention of the public and a reasonable fee may be charged for providing a copy. A copy of the statement must also be given without delay to the Treasury. The Authority must also publish a revised statement if it decides to change the procedures. Under *subsection (9)* the Authority must act in accordance with its published procedures. *Subsection (11)* ensures that the validity of any notices given in such a case is not affected by any failure to do so. However, *subsection (12)* makes clear that the Tribunal can take into account any failure to follow the procedures.

Section 396: ***Statements under*** *section 395*

698. This section makes provision about consultation arrangements. These are similar to those in other equivalent provisions of the Act, such as under section 70 to the issuing of a statement under section 395.

Part Xxvii: Offences

699. This Part contains provisions which make it an offence to make misleading statements or engage in a misleading practice in order to induce someone to enter into an investment contract. It also creates offences of misleading the Authority and the DGFT. The first of these offences is carried over from sections 47 and 133 of the FS Act 1986 and section 35 of the Banking Act. It also provides that where a corporate body (or partnership) has committed an offence then, in certain circumstances, its officers may also be guilty of that offence. In addition, this Part contains general provisions on the institution of proceedings for offences under this Act. It gives the Authority powers to prosecute insider dealing under the Criminal Justice Act 1993, to prosecute under the Money Laundering Regulations 1993, and to prosecute the offences of misleading statements and practices.

Section 397: Misleading statements and practices

700. This section provides for two criminal offences concerning misleading statements and practices. Persons found guilty of either of these offences may be subject to a maximum of up to 7 years imprisonment or to a fine, or to both.

701. The first, set out in *subsections (1) and (2),* applies where a person deliberately makes a misleading statement, promise or forecast, or dishonestly conceals facts from someone with the intention of inducing any other person to do or refrain from doing something in relation to an investment. A possible example of this offence would be someone lying about a company's financial position at a time when he was seeking to dispose of shares in that company. It is also an offence to make the misleading statement, promise or forecast recklessly and to be reckless as to whether another person was so induced.

702. The second offence, set out in *subsection (3)*, is the creation of a misleading impression about an investment with the intention of inducing another person to do or not do something in relation to that investment. This covers such things as market manipulation, for example engaging in artificial trades in a particular investment in order to create the impression that there is more interest in the investment than really exists.

703. *Subsection (4)* provides a defence against the offence in *subsection (2)* for a person if he can show that a statement, promise or forecast was made in compliance with price stabilising or control of information rules. *Subsection (5)* provides three defences against the offence in *subsection (3).* The first is that the person concerned reasonably believed that his conduct would not create a misleading impression. The second defence is where the person is engaged in price stabilisation in circumstances where this is permitted. The third defence is where the person acted in conformity with the control of information rules under section 147.

704. *Subsection (7)* provides the offence in *subsection (3)* is not committed unless the action done takes place in the United Kingdom, or the misleading impression this creates arises in the United Kingdom.

705. *Subsections (9) to (12)* give the Treasury the power to prescribe those agreements and investments to which this section applies.

Section 398: Misleading the Authority: residual cases

706. This section makes it an offence to give false or misleading information to the Authority in purported compliance with requirements under the Act in cases where this is not already an offence under other provisions (for example under section 177(4) regarding the provision of information to investigators). The penalty for this offence is an unlimited fine on indictment or a fine of up to the statutory maximum (£5,000) on summary conviction.

Section 399: Misleading the Director General of Fair Trading

707. This section applies the provisions of section 44 of the Competition Act 1998. The effect of this is that it is an offence to mislead or give false information to the DGFT when he is exercising his functions under the Act.

Section 400: Offences by bodies corporate etc.

708. This section makes provision as to the circumstances in which partners in a partnership and directors and officers of bodies corporate and unincorporated associations may be found guilty of an offence in a case in which an offence has been committed by the relevant partnership, body or association.

709. *Subsection (7)* gives the Treasury the power to make regulations applying the provisions of this section, with any appropriate modifications, to equivalent undertakings established under the laws of other countries.

Section 401: Proceedings for offences

710. This section confers powers to prosecute offences under this Act. The Secretary of State and the Authority can prosecute any offence in England, Wales or Northern Ireland. Others can only prosecute with the consent of the Director of Public Prosecutions in England and Wales or, in Northern Ireland, with the consent of the Director of Public Prosecutions for Northern Ireland. The DGFT can prosecute in England, Wales or Northern Ireland for breaches of any prohibition on carrying on any CCA 1974 business he has imposed under section 203.

711. *Subsections (5) and (6)* give the Treasury the power to set conditions relating to the way in which the Authority can bring proceedings for offences under this Act. For example, the Treasury could require the Authority to comply with the Code for Crown Prosecutors. In Scotland, prosecution will be the responsibility of the Lord Advocate.

Section 402: Power of the Authority to institute proceedings for certain other offences

712. This section allows the Authority to prosecute in England, Wales or Northern Ireland two criminal offences which are not in this Act. These are the offences of insider dealing (Part V of the Criminal Justice Act 1993) and breach of the Money Laundering Regulations 1993 (regulation 5).

713. *Subsections (2) and (3)* give the Treasury the power to set conditions relating to the way in which the Authority can bring proceedings for these offences. For example, the Treasury could require the Authority to comply with the Code for Crown Prosecutors.

Section 403: Jurisdiction and procedure in respect of certain offences

714. This section makes provision for the procedures under which offences under the Act may be prosecuted and punished. It carries forward and has similar effect to the provisions of section 203 of the Financial Services Act 1986.

715. *Subsection (1)* makes clear that a fine imposed upon a unincorporated association must be paid out of the funds of the association, whilst *subsection (2)* provides that any proceedings for an offence brought against an unincorporated association must be brought in the name of the association. *Subsections (3) and (4)* provide that for the purposes of the service of documents, and of prosecutions, unincorporated associations should be treated in the same way as bodies corporate. *Subsection (5)* provides that summary proceedings may be taken against a body corporate or unincorporated association at their place of business, whilst proceedings may be brought against an individual at any place where he is present for the time being.

Part Xxviii: Miscellaneous

Section 404: Schemes for reviewing past business

716. This section enables the Treasury, by order under *subsection (2)*, to set out the framework for a scheme to be established and operated by the Authority to require authorised persons to review their past business and, where appropriate, to determine the amounts payable by those persons by way of compensation for liabilities that they have incurred to private investors and certain others. This power will facilitate the handling of issues such as those which arose in cases of mis-selling - most notably of personal pensions.

Reciprocity powers

717. Sections 405 to 408 concern reciprocity powers. Under certain EC directives a decision can be taken by the Council of the European Union or the Commission to require individual member States' regulators to take reciprocal action to deprive subsidiaries of firms from a country outside the European Economic Area (EEA) of access to their markets. This is referred to in the Act as a "third country decision". Such a decision may be taken where it appears to the Commission that EEA firms wishing to establish themselves or provide financial services in third countries are not being treated on the same basis and offered the same competitive opportunities as domestic firms.

718. The potential for reciprocity action has diminished following World Trade Organisation ("WTO") negotiations on financial services which resulted in the EU, along with many other WTO member countries, making a commitment to offer Most Favoured Nation treatment to other WTO members on a permanent basis. This commitment came into force on 1 March 1999 and means that EC reciprocity powers can now only be used against countries outside the WTO.

*Section 405: **Directions***

719. This section defines the nature of reciprocity action that may be taken in order to comply with a third country decision. The section provides the Treasury with the power to direct the Authority to do the following:

- refuse, or put on hold, an application for authorisation from a person which is formed under the law of the United Kingdom but which is the direct or indirect subsidiary (the powers do not apply to branches) of a firm from a country which is the subject of a third country decision (*subsections (1)(a) and (b)*);
- object to a person from a country which is the subject of a third country decision acquiring a 50 per cent share in an authorised person incorporated in the United Kingdom or formed under UK law whether or not they have served the Authority with a notice of control as required under Part XII (*subsections (1)(c) and (d)*)

720. The circumstances in which a person is taken to acquire a 50 per cent share is defined in section 406.

*Section 407: **Consequences of a direction under** section 405*

721. This section sets out the procedure the Authority must follow if the Treasury directs them to implement a third country decision.

*Section 408: **EFTA firms***

722. If a subsidiary of a firm from a country subject to a third country decision is already authorised in an EU member State then its entitlement to exercise passport rights (see explanatory notes to Schedule 3) to establish a branch or provide services in another member State is not affected if by the third country decision. This is not the case for subsidiaries of third country firms authorised in EEA States which are not also EU member States (Norway, Iceland or Liechtenstein), referred to in the Act as "EFTA firms" (*subsection (8)*). EFTA firms may not exercise their passport rights following a third country decision relating to the country of their parent. This section therefore gives the Treasury the power to make a determination that a particular firm does, or class of firms do, not qualify for authorisation under Schedule 3. *Subsections (6) and (7)* set out the procedure the Treasury must follow if it makes such a determination.

*Section 409: **Gibraltar***

723. This section provides for matters arising from Gibraltar's status within the EEA.

724. *Subsection (1)(a)* gives the Treasury the power to extend Schedule 3 so that Gibraltar firms which are covered by one of the single market directives to which effect has been given in Gibraltar would be able to qualify for status as an authorised person and establish a branch or provide services within the United Kingdom. It also enables the Treasury to make the necessary provision to ensure that firms from other EEA States which exercise passport rights in relation to Gibraltar before they exercise them in relation to the United Kingdom proper are not required unnecessarily to duplicate notification requirements.

725. *Subsection (1)(d)* does the equivalent for Gibraltar based collective investment schemes. The Treasury also has the power under *subsection (1)(c)* to extend the application of Schedule 4 so that a financial services firm with its head office in Gibraltar or being otherwise connected with Gibraltar would acquire Treaty rights if it is authorised by the Gibraltar competent authority and the relevant conditions in Schedule 4 are met.

726. *Subsection (1)(e)* will enable the Treasury to modify the provisions of section 264 so that the Authority can refuse to admit a collective investment scheme from another member State if the way in which it proposes to market its units is incompatible with requirements imposed in Gibraltar in the general good.

727. *Subsection (1)(b)* gives the Treasury the power, by order, to extend the application of Schedule 3 to the Act so as to make provision as to the exercise by UK firms of rights which are afforded to them under the law of Gibraltar which corresponds to an EEA right.

Section 410: ***International obligations***

728. This section provides the Treasury with the general power to direct a number of bodies with powers under the Act to take, or refrain from taking, any action which is either required by, or is incompatible with, the United Kingdom's international obligations. For example, if the Authority's rules on capital requirements were such that the UK's obligations under EC law were not being met, this section would allow the Treasury to direct the Authority to change their rules so as to ensure compliance.

Section 411: ***Tax treatment of levies and repayments***

729. This section relates to levies and payments relating to the legal assistance scheme under Part IX, the compensation scheme under Part XV and the ombudsman scheme under Part XVI. This section amends the Income and Corporation Taxes Act 1988 so that it provides for such levies to be treated as a tax deductible expense and for levy rebates made to authorised persons to be treated as trading receipts.

Section 412: ***Gaming contracts***

730. Legislation governing gaming contracts includes provisions for such contracts not to be legally enforceable. Some regulated activities involve entering into or performing contracts which could potentially be covered by this legislation, for example derivative contracts such as "put options", and the effect of this section is to make certain that such contracts are legally enforceable.

Section 413: ***Protected items***

731. This section provides that no power under the Act can be used to require any person to produce, disclose or permit the inspection of "protected items". These are defined in terms which are materially identical to the definition of items subject to legal professional privilege in section 10 of the Police and Criminal Evidence Act 1984.

Section 414: Service of notices

732. This section enables the Treasury to make regulations prescribing the procedure for giving notices and other documents under the Act. The power covers any such provision in the Act, regardless of its precise wording, and includes provisions about giving directions or imposing requirements.

733. In particular, the regulations may specify how a document may be given, the address to which it should be sent, and whether the document or notice may be sent electronically. They may also specify the date and time a document is to be regarded as having been served (this may be important, for example, where a time limit begins to run from that date). The regulations may also make particular provision for cases where the person to whom the document is being sent is not an individual (for example, in the case of a limited company or partnership) or is outside the United Kingdom. The precise arrangements required under the regulations may vary depending on the nature of the document in question.

Section 415: Jurisdiction in civil proceedings

734. This section enables civil proceedings, such as judicial review, to be brought against any of the bodies corporate on which functions are conferred by this Act in the courts of any part of the United Kingdom. This is necessary because these bodies are companies incorporated under the Companies Acts and, as such, the effect of the Civil Jurisdiction and Judgments Act 1982 would otherwise be that civil proceedings could be brought against them only in the courts in England and Wales because that is the part of the United Kingdom in which they are treated as being domiciled for the purposes of that Act. That Act is amended by paragraph 3 of Schedule 20.

Section 416: Provisions relating to industrial assurance and certain other enactments

735. This section provides for the Industrial Assurance Acts 1923-48 (and the equivalent Northern Ireland Order) to cease to have effect and for the repeal of the Insurance Brokers (Registration) Act 1977. It also provides for the dissolution of certain statutory bodies mentioned in *subsection (3)*. The section also confers on the Treasury a power by order to make such provisions as it considers necessary in consequence of the provisions of this section. Such consequential provisions would allow, for example, for the protection of existing policyholders under the Industrial Assurance Acts, and to make provision for the orderly dissolution of the bodies mentioned.

736. The repeals and dissolutions set out in this section are dealt with on the face of the Act because they may not be entirely consequential on the other provisions of the Act and therefore maybe outside the scope of section 426, which allows for consequential repeals to be made by order.

Part Xxix: Interpretation

737. This Part defines a number of the terms used in the Act. The majority of such definitions are contained in section 417.

Section 418: Carrying on regulated activities in the United Kingdom

738. This section deals with the territorial scope of the authorisation requirement, and establishes its so-called "outward"#application, whereby persons based in the United Kingdom who carry on regulated activities overseas need to be regulated in the United Kingdom. The section reflects the provisions of the EC directives in determining when a person is to be considered to be carrying on regulated activities in the United Kingdom, and sets out four broad cases:

- first, all persons who have their head or registered office in the United Kingdom, but who only carry on regulated activities in another EEA State, but are entitled to exercise rights under a single market directive as UK firms, and are carrying on in another EEA state regulated activities to which that directive applies, will need to be authorised in the United Kingdom;
- second, all persons who have their registered offices (or head offices, where they do not have registered offices) in the United Kingdom, and operate as managers of schemes which are entitled to enjoy the rights conferred by a relevant Community Instrument will require authorisation where persons in another EEA state are invited to become participants in the schemes;
- third, all persons who have their head or registered office in the United Kingdom, but who only carry on regulated activities in non-EEA states, will need to be authorised if they direct the day-to-day management of the activities from an establishment in the United Kingdom; or
- fourth, even if a person does not have a head or registered office in the United Kingdom and is not dealing with UK customers, he will still need to be authorised if the activity is carried on from an establishment maintained by him in the United Kingdom.

739. These provisions complement the so-called "inward" territorial scope of the Act, whereby overseas persons who carry on regulated activities in the United Kingdom need to be regulated unless an exemption or exclusion applies. The "inward" scope of the Act is implicit in the terms of section 19, but it may also be further amplified or restricted by the order to be made under section 22.

*Section 419: **Carrying on regulated activities by way of business***

740. This section allows the Treasury to make orders to define "carrying on a regulated activity by way of business" for the purposes of section 22. This would, for example, allow special provision to be made in the case of occupational pension schemes, as under the FS Act 1986. The section would also enable different provision to be made in the case of different activities, if that was thought to be desirable in the light of the slightly different tests which apply under the existing legislation.

*Section 420: **Parent and subsidiary undertaking***

741. The definitions of parent and subsidiary undertaking for the purposes of the Act are consistent with the definitions used in the single market directives.

742. Although individuals are not themselves "undertakings", it is possible for an individual to have a relationship with an undertaking which would be classified as a parent/ subsidiary relationship if they were an undertaking. *Subsection (2)* clarifies that for the purposes of the Act such an individual is to be included as a parent undertaking. The undertaking with whom the individual has a parent/subsidiary relationship is to be included as a subsidiary undertaking.

743. *Subsection (2)* also extends the definitions in relation to EEA bodies to cover any undertaking which would be treated as a parent or subsidiary undertaking under the law of the EEA state where the body is established.

Part Xxx: Supplemental

744. This Part contains various supplemental provisions. For example, provisions as to Parliamentary control over statutory instruments and provisions enabling the Treasury to make transitional provisions and consequential amendments. It also determines the name by which the Act may be cited.

Section 426: Consequential and supplementary provision

745. This section confers on Ministers of the Crown a power, exercisable by order, to make incidental, consequential, transitional or supplemental provisions. The provisions which may be made include ones which appear to the Ministers to be necessary or expedient in order to give full effect to the Act. This power will be used in particular to make consequential amendments and repeals to other legislation when the Act is brought into force.

Section 427: Transitional provisions

746. This section amplifies the power conferred on Ministers of the Crown by section 426, permitting an order under that section may make particular provision in respect of transitional matters or savings. The complexity of the transition to the regulatory regime to be established under this Act is such that it may be necessary to make provisions of the kinds described in this section which might not otherwise fall within the scope of section 426.

747. For example, *subsection (2)(a)* makes clear that an order under section 426 could provide for a person authorised under predecessor arrangements to have permission from the day the relevant provisions of this Act come into force to continue to carry on the activities permitted by the authorisation from the predecessor regulator. An order under section 426 may also make provision for the continuation of rules and regulations. It is expected that most rules made by the Authority will be new rules made for the purposes of the Act. However, there may be a need for the continuation of rules under previous legislation, at least for a transitional period. This section will enable the Authority to be given power to carry forward such rules and regulations which it could make under this Act. This section also provides that an order under section 426 may deal with disciplinary cases in train on the day of commencement, and for transitional provisions to be made in respect of ombudsman and compensation schemes.

Section 429: Parliamentary control of statutory instruments

748. This section sets out the procedure for making statutory instruments under the powers in the Act. Most of the powers to make orders and regulations under the Act are subject to the negative resolution procedure. The power to appoint a day for the commencement of particular provisions of the Act under section 431(2) is not subject to Parliamentary control. However, the affirmative procedure applies to the following powers:

- the power initially to set the definition, or to extend the scope of, regulated activities under section 22(1) (the type of affirmative procedure applicable to this power is set out in paragraph 26 of Schedule 2);
- the power initially to specify the matters set out in section 21(4), (5), (9) and (10) (the meaning of certain elements of the basic restriction on financial promotion and the exceptions from that restriction);
- any subsequent exercise of the power to specify the matters dealt with in section 21(4) and (5) (the meaning of certain elements of the basic restriction on financial promotion) which has the effect of extending that restriction so as to apply in circumstances in which it did not previously apply;
- the power to add to the activities and investments that are “controlled” for the purposes of section 21;
- the power under section 38, when it is first used, and any subsequent exercise of the power that has the effect of restricting or removing an exemption previously conferred by an order under section 38;
- the power to set the scope of price stabilising rules under section 144(4);

- the power under section 192(b) to vary, remove from or add to the cases in which a person has control for the purposes of Part XII and the equivalent power in section 192(e) in relation to the meaning of "controller" in section 422;
- the power under section 236(5) to amend the definition of open-ended investment company;
- the power for the establishment and regulation of collective investment schemes in Great Britain taking the form of oeics under section 262;
- the power initially to determine the circumstances in which the carrying on of regulated activities by members of the professions is subject to the arrangements set out under section 326(1) and restriction of exemption from the general prohibition under section 327(6)) and any subsequent exercise of those powers so as to restrict those circumstances;
- the power under section 404 authorising a scheme for reviewing past business;
- an order under section 419 defining the business test; and
- the power under paragraph 1 of Schedule 8 to allow any exercisable function conferred on the competent authority to be transferred in order for another person to exercise that function.

Schedule 1: the Financial Services Authority

749. Part I of this Schedule sets out requirements for the Authority's constitution and imposes certain obligations on it. Part II deals with the status of the Authority. Parts III and IV concern the Authority's powers to raise fees and impose penalties and certain other matters. Part IV gives the Authority and those who work for it limited immunity from suit.

Part I: General

Paragraph 2: Constitution

750. This paragraph requires the Authority to have a chairman and a governing body which includes the chairman. Both the chairman and the members of the governing body must be appointed and be liable to removal from office by the Treasury.

751. *Sub-paragraph (4)* provides for the acts of the Authority still to be valid irrespective of a vacancy in the office of chairman or any defect in an appointment to the governing body. This is to prevent the Authority's rules, and any action it takes in pursuit of its functions, being rendered invalid purely as a result of such a vacancy or defect.

Paragraph 3: Non-executive members of the governing body

752. This paragraph provides that the Authority's governing body must include a majority of non-executive members and requires there to be a committee of the non-executive members of the governing body, the chairman of which is to be appointed by the Treasury.

Paragraph 4: Functions of the non-executive committee

753. The functions of the non-executive members are not restricted by the non-executive committee. The non-executive committee has three specified functions. These are:

- keeping under review the efficiency and economy with which the Authority uses its resources;
- keeping under review its internal financial controls; and

- determining the remuneration of the chairman and the executive members of the governing body.

754. The committee's function of keeping the Authority's economic and efficient use of its resources under review must be undertaken by the whole committee. However, the function of reviewing internal financial controls and determining the remuneration of the chairman and executive members of the governing body may be performed by a sub-committee.

*Paragraph 5: **Arrangements for discharging functions***

755. This paragraph allows the Authority's functions, with the exception of its legislative functions, to be delegated below the level of the governing body. The legislative functions are rule-making, giving general guidance, issuing statements, issuing codes, and giving directions.

*Paragraph 6: **Monitoring and enforcement***

756. This paragraph requires the Authority to maintain arrangements for monitoring compliance with, and enforcing requirements imposed by or under, the Act. The Authority may arrange for monitoring, but not enforcement, to be delegated to another body or person which it believes is competent, which might include, for example, a professional body. If it does so, the Authority remains responsible for ensuring that proper monitoring arrangements are in place.

*Paragraph 7: **Arrangements for the investigation of complaints***

757. The Authority is required to put in place a scheme, the "complaints scheme", for the prompt, independent investigation of complaints made against it. These might typically be complaints about maladministraton by the Authority.

758. *Sub-paragraphs (1), (2) and (3)* require the Authority to establish a complaints scheme and appoint an independent investigator, whose appointment and removal will be subject to the approval of the Treasury.

759. *Sub-paragraph (4)* requires the investigator be appointed on terms and conditions reasonably designed to ensure his independence from the Authority and to ensure that complaints will be investigated under the scheme without favouring the Authority.

760. *Sub-paragraphs (5) to (9) and (14)* provide for the Authority to consult on its proposals for the complaints scheme.

761. *Sub-paragraph (10) to (13)* provide that the Authority is required to publish details of the complaints scheme and the powers of the independent investigator. The Authority may charge a reasonable fee for providing a person with a copy of details published under this paragraph.

*Paragraph 8: **Investigation of complaints***

762. This paragraph is concerned with the operation of the complaints scheme. The Authority may decide not to investigate a complaint in accordance with the scheme where it considers that the complaint would more appropriately be dealt with in another way, for example by reference to the Tribunal.

763. Under *sub-paragraph (2)*, the Authority is required to ensure that the independent investigator has the means at his disposal to conduct a full investigation of complaints referred to him, and the investigator can publish his report if he considers that the matter ought to be brought to the attention of the public. The investigator may, *under sub-paragraphs (3) and (4)*, choose to investigate complaints in accordance with the scheme which the Authority has, itself, declined to pursue. If a report is critical of the

Authority, *sub-paragraphs (6) and (7)* require the Authority to inform the investigator and the complainant of the steps it proposes to take in response, and the investigator may require the Authority to publish all or part of that response. *Sub-paragraph (5)* requires that the scheme allows the investigator to recommend that the Authority makes a compensatory payment to the complainant or remedies the matter, or both. *Sub-paragraph (9)* prevents an officer or employee of the Authority from investigating a complaint on the investigator's behalf.

*Paragraph 9: **Records***

764. The Authority must have satisfactory arrangements for recording its decisions and for the safe-keeping of those records which it considers should be preserved.

*Paragraph 10: **Annual report***

765. This requires the Authority to report at least once a year to the Treasury on the discharge of its functions and, in particular, the extent to which the statutory objectives have been met and its regulatory principles under section 2(3) have been taken into account and such other matters as directed by the Treasury. It also requires the Treasury to lay the report before Parliament.

766. *Sub-paragraph (2)* requires that the report of the Authority must be accompanied by a report by the non-executive members of the governing body and allows the Treasury to direct that any other reports or information, including material prepared by third parties such as an auditor's report, also accompany it.

767. *Sub-paragraphs (4) to (6)* allow the Treasury to direct the Authority to comply with provisions of the Companies Act which would otherwise not apply to it dealing with accounts and their audit. The direction may modify provisions under that Act in their application to the Authority. This is to ensure that the Authority is required to prepare audited accounts which are open to inspection irrespective of any exemptions which are made under that Act which would otherwise apply to the Authority.

*Paragraph 11: **Annual public meeting***

768. The Authority must hold an annual public meeting to consider the most recent report of the Authority, within three months of its publication. The meeting should allow for a general discussion of the contents of the annual report and give those attending an opportunity to put questions to the Authority on the discharge of its functions. Paragraph 12 requires the Authority to publish a report of the proceedings of the meeting.

Part II: Status

*Paragraphs 14 and 15: **Exemption from requirement of "limited" in Authority's name***

769. The Authority is a company limited by guarantee. These paragraphs exempt the Authority from having to include "limited" in its name, as would normally be required under the Companies Act. They also provide for the Secretary of State to remove that exemption if it is inappropriate for it to continue.

Part III: Fees

*Paragraph 16: **Penalties***

770. This paragraph provides that in determining its policy with regard to the level of penalties to impose under powers in the Act, the Authority may take no account of its expenses or anticipated expenses. It clarifies that there is to be no link or incentive to fund the Authority by levying penalties on the regulated community.

771. *Sub-paragraph (2)* requires the Authority to operate a scheme to ensure that penalties paid to the Authority are to be applied for the benefit of authorised persons. The Authority is required to consult on these arrangements.

*Paragraph 17: **Fees***

772. This provides for a rule-making power for the Authority to raise fees for what it does in the discharge of its functions under the Act. It may use the fees to meet its expenses, to repay borrowing incurred in preparing for the assumption of functions under the Act and by virtue of the Bank of England Act 1998 and to maintain adequate reserves.

773. The Authority may not take into account any penalties which it has received, or expects to receive, in setting the fees under the Act.

*Paragraph 18: **Services for which fees may not be charged***

774. Fees may not be charged when a person gives notice of their intention to exercise passporting rights under Schedule 3 or to persons approved under the employed persons regime in Part V.

Part IV: Miscellaneous

*Paragraph 19: **Exemption from liability in damages***

775. This paragraph provides immunity for the Authority and its staff from actions for damages except where they act in bad faith or where damages are sought under the Human Rights Act 1998. Similar immunity is granted to the independent investigator appointed under paragraph 7.

*Paragraph 20: **Disqualification for membership of House of Commons***

776. Serving members of the Authority's board are disqualified from membership of the House of Commons. Paragraph 19 makes similar provision in respect of the Northern Ireland Assembly. Provision in respect of the Scottish Parliament and the Welsh Assembly are made respectively in the Scotland Act 1998 and the Government of Wales Act 1998.

*Schedule 2: **Regulated Activities***

777. This Schedule does not define what activities are regulated under the Act. The regulated activities will be those activities which are prescribed using the power conferred by section 22. The Schedule sets out a list of "activities" and "investments" which, together, indicate the broad scope of activities which are potentially regulated under the Act. The scope of the Act is not strictly limited by the Schedule, but rather by the overall object and purpose of the Act. However, the general nature of the activities set out in the Schedule serves to inform and therefore indirectly limit the extent of the Treasury's power to bring further activities within the scope of the Act.

778. It is within this overall object and purpose that the power under section 22 to prescribe the regulated activities operates. Orders made under that section will be an exhaustive statement of the regulated activities.

779. The Schedule is in three parts. The first Part describes certain activities which when carried on in relation to "investments" may be regulated. The second describes the "investments". The third makes further provisions as to the scope of the order-making power under section 22.

780. The activities, which in each case include offering or agreeing to carry on the activity as well as actually carrying it out, are:

- dealing in investments, which includes buying, selling, subscribing for or underwriting investments. It covers a person acting as either principal or agent. In relation to insurance, dealing also includes carrying out a contract of insurance;
- arranging deals in investments on behalf of others, or making arrangements which enable other persons to deal;
- accepting deposits;
- safeguarding or administering assets for another person, or arranging for their assets to be safeguarded or administered;
- managing assets on behalf of another person, where those assets are or may include investments;
- giving advice on the buying, selling, subscribing for or underwriting of an investment or about the exercise of any right conferred by an investment to buy or sell, subscribe or otherwise convert an investment (examples of conversions on which advice might be given would include a corporate bond which, in certain circumstances, could be converted into, or redeemed in return for, a share of the equity in the company concerned);
- establishing, operating or winding up a collective investment scheme, including acting as trustee, or depositary or sole director of certain types of scheme;
- sending, or causing to be sent, instructions by means of a computer based system as to the transfer of investments. This element would cover computer-based clearing systems such as that operated by CREST.

781. Part II of the Schedule is an indicative list of the investments relevant to the question whether an activity could be brought within regulation under section 22. These are:

- stocks and shares in companies incorporated in the United Kingdom or elsewhere, or in unincorporated bodies constituted under the law of any territory;
- instruments creating or acknowledging indebtedness, such as loan stock, certificates of deposit, debentures and bonds, including debt issued by Governments, local authorities or international organizations of which the United Kingdom or any other EU member State is a member, such as the United Nations or the OECD;
- instruments, such as warrants, conferring a right to subscribe in other types of investment (including investments which are not yet in existence or which, like ordinary shares in a company, are not individually identifiable);
- instruments which confer contractual or property rights to underlying investments and which can be traded or transferred without reference to the party holding the underlying investments. Explicit inclusion of this element reflects the established practice whereby a public issue of securities might be made by issuing the securities themselves to a third party, which would issue certificates (which may confer only a proportionate property right to a security) to the subscribing public, which are then tradable as if they were the underlying securities themselves;
- units in, or securities issued by, collective investment schemes and open-ended investment companies;
- options to buy or sell property;
- futures, which are contractual rights to buy or sell a commodity or property at a future date and at a price agreed at the time that the contract is made (though the price might still be contingent on other factors). This includes both bilateral

"forward" contracts as well as standardized futures contracts traded on a futures exchange such as London International Financial Futures Exchange ("LIFFE");

- contracts for differences and other contracts whose value depends on fluctuations in the value of some factor such as property or index, for example interest rate swaps;
- contracts of insurance;
- membership and potential membership of a Lloyd's syndicate and the underwriting capacity of such a syndicate;
- deposits, that is contracts under which money is paid other than in return for goods or services and on the basis that it will be repaid, with or without interest, on demand or at some specified times or circumstances;
- loans secured on land, such as mortgages; and
- any other right or interest in any other investment.

782. Part III makes provision as to the scope of the order-making power under section 22. The first order to be made under that section must be subject to an affirmative resolution procedure - that is, it must be laid before Parliament after being made, and it will cease to have effect if it is not approved by a resolution of each House within 28 days of being made. The same procedure will apply where an order under section 22 has the effect of extending the scope of activities to be regulated under the Act.

*Schedule 3: **Eea Passport Rights***

783. This Schedule gives effect in UK law to the single markets in banking, investment services and insurance as provided for by the relevant directives: the 2nd Banking Co-ordination Directive, the Investment Services Directive and the Life and Non-Life Directives.

784. Under the directives, credit institutions (a term embracing both banks and building societies), investment firms and insurance companies (which includes friendly societies) with head offices in any member State of EEA (that is the 15 States of the EU plus Norway, Iceland and Liechtenstein) have rights to carry on certain activities in other member States by virtue of their home State authorisation. These rights are often referred to as their "passport" and cover a range of financial services (some of which may only be conducted by firms which are authorised under these categories), which include deposit-taking, effecting and carrying out life or general insurance.

785. Under the 2nd Banking Co-ordination Directive, subsidiaries of credit institutions which meet certain criteria set out in article 18(2) of that directive may also have passport rights, and are therefore included in the definitions of "EEA firms" (persons from other member States who qualify for the passport into the United Kingdom) and "UK firms" (persons established in the United Kingdom who exercise their passport rights in other member States) in this Schedule.

786. The authorities in the member States, other than the home State, where these passporters are carrying on business under their passports (referred to as the host State authorities) may only impose limited regulations on the conduct of business under the passport, in accordance with the established principle of the "general good". This requires those rules to be proportionate, non-discriminatory and non-duplicative of home State rules with equivalent effect. Conduct of business rules generally come within the host State remit. The home State retains full responsibility for authorising the passporting firms and conducting their overall prudential supervision (that is, supervising their financial soundness and ensuring that they and their controllers are fit and proper to conduct such business).

787. The passport may be exercised in order to establish a permanent place of business, referred to in the directives as a "branch" irrespective of the number of sites involved, or in order to provide cross-border services without a permanent place of business. Indeed the passport may be exercised in order to provide services, perhaps different services, by these two means in parallel.

788. The business activities covered by the passport do not necessarily correspond exactly to the activities which are regulated under the law of any member State, although certain activities, such as deposit-taking, insurance business or the core investment services defined under the Investment Services Directive, must be regulated, and will all be regulated activities under the order made under section 22. There are therefore activities for which firms may have rights to conduct in other member States by virtue of the passport, but which are not necessarily central to the definition of those firms which qualify for the passport. There may equally be activities which are covered by the passport, but which are not regulated activities in every member State.

789. An example of an activity not regulated in every member State is lending. Lending, in conjunction with deposit-taking, is a defining characteristic of what is a credit institution and therefore of those who may qualify for passport rights under the 2nd Banking Co-ordination Directive. However, the directives do not require that lending should be regulated, though they do require the regulation of deposit-taking. The passport under that directive therefore not only covers lending, but qualification for that passport depends on it being part of the business of the firm. However, lending is not covered by the other directives (indeed, insurance companies are prohibited from carrying on the business of lending unless it is ancillary to their insurance business) and it does not need to be regulated by member States. It is not currently a regulated activity in the United Kingdom, except to the extent that it falls within the scope of the CCA 1974.

790. This Schedule, in conjunction with section 31, therefore defines the firms from other EEA member States, which may qualify for authorisation via this route, and the procedures which, in accordance with the various directives, must be followed (see paragraphs 12 to 14 in Part II). An EEA firm which fails to follow the correct notification procedure does not, however, commit an offence and their contracts are not rendered unenforceable in consequence (see paragraph 16).

791. Part III of the Schedule gives effect to the outward passport entitlements of UK credit institutions, investment firms and insurance companies. For the reasons referred to above, those qualifying for the passport form a narrower class than all persons who have their head office in the United Kingdom and who are authorised by virtue of having a Part IV permission. For example, not all banks and building societies are necessarily credit institutions, though the vast majority are. Equally the definition of an investment firm for the purposes of the Investment Services Directive is restricted to a firm which is authorised to carry on the business of providing for third parties the core services defined under that directive.

792. Paragraphs 19 and 20 set out the procedure and conditions on which the Authority may grant the passport to those UK firms who qualify. A UK firm which fails to follow the required notification procedures before establishing a branch or providing services in another member State commits an offence under paragraph 21.

793. The Schedule also gives the Treasury powers to make regulations governing the continuing regulation of both EEA firms and UK firms.

794. Paragraph 23 enables the Authority to intervene in respect of a UK firm's consumer credit business in another member State. Paragraph 24 similarly enables the Authority to intervene in the business carried on in other member States of subsidiaries qualifying for the outward passport under Article 18(2) of the 2nd Banking Co-ordination Directive. Such subsidiaries need not be authorised persons in their own right.

Schedule 4: Treaty Rights

795. This Schedule gives effect in UK law to the rights of establishment and to provide services of persons established in the other EEA States. These relate to rights which go beyond those which are covered by the single market directives in banking, investment services and insurance (see Schedule 3).

796. These rights allow persons who are authorised under the law of one member State to carry on an activity in the other member States so long as the relevant law of the home State provides equivalent protection to that of the host State and meets any EU minimum requirements applicable in that area of law. These rights are given precise effect for many financial services firms through the single market directives, and the member State laws giving national effect to them. However, as explained in relation to Schedule 3, the directives do not cover the full range of financial services or financial service providers. It is necessary, therefore, to provide an equivalent mechanism to permit persons from other EU member States to exercise their Treaty rights in the absence of formal directive passporting arrangements. The provisions in this Schedule, in conjunction with section 31, provide for that mechanism.

797. The Schedule does not seek to define the extent of Treaty rights, which are in any event the subject of extensive and developing case law in the EU, but sets the conditions that must be met for authorisation by this route in terms of the general principles described above. It requires home State confirmation of a firm's home State authorisation and provides for the Treasury to take the decision as to whether the particular laws of a particular member State provide the equivalent protection required.

798. The firm is also required to give notice of their intention to exercise their Treaty rights and to provide such information as the Authority may require. Failure to give proper notice is a criminal offence, unless all reasonable precautions have been taken to avoid the commission of the offence. It is also an offence knowingly or recklessly to provide false or misleading information.

Schedule 5: Persons Concerned in Collective Investment Schemes

799. This schedule effectively deals with authorisation of collective investment schemes in two circumstances:

- first, it affords authorisation to incoming passporters under the relevant directives, and
- second, it deals with authorisation for certain types of oeic. The Treasury may prescribe additional conditions for qualification for automatic authorisation. A person who is authorised under this Schedule has permission to carry on regulated activities in connection with the scheme of which he is the operator or depositary.

Schedule 6: Threshold Conditions

Part I: Part IV Permission

800. This Part sets out the minimum conditions against which an applicant for permission under section 40 must be measured. Failure to meet one of the conditions is sufficient grounds for refusal to grant permission or for granting permission for a narrower range or definition of regulated activities than sought by the applicant. However, the fact that an applicant satisfies all the applicable conditions in this Schedule does not confer any automatic right to permission. The Authority retains some discretion to refuse an application even where all these conditions are satisfied.

801. The conditions must also be met on an on-going basis by authorised persons and failure to meet one of the conditions is sufficient grounds for the exercise by the Authority of its power to vary an authorised person's permission under section 45, and through that power, its power to withdraw an authorised person's authorisation under

section 33. However, the Authority may, from time to time, temporarily subordinate the need to ensure that the threshold conditions are met on a continuous basis in line with its statutory objective of protecting consumers.

*Paragraph 1: **Legal Status***

802. This paragraph sets out certain conditions for legal form. Section 40 allows for authorised persons to be natural persons as well as companies, partnerships or other unincorporated associations. However, not all these forms are acceptable under EC law for authorised persons carrying on certain types of business.

803. Thus the effecting and carrying out of contracts of insurance is limited to bodies corporate, registered friendly societies or members of Lloyd's insurance market, and only bodies corporate or partnerships may accept deposits.

*Paragraph 2: **Location of offices***

804. This paragraph implements the requirement under the Post-BCCI Directive (Council Directive 95/26/EEC of 29 June 1995) that persons covered by the single market directive should have their head office in the country in which they have their registered office. It requires authorised persons who are bodies corporate constituted under the law of any part of the United Kingdom, to have their head office (that is, the main centre from which the firm is run) in the United Kingdom. If they have a registered office, as most bodies corporate do, it must also be in the United Kingdom. If the person does not have a registered office (for instance if he is an individual or an unincorporated association) but his head office is in the United Kingdom, he must carry on authorisable business in the United Kingdom. This requirement is aimed at ensuring that authorised persons organise their business in a way that can be effectively supervised. A problem in the case of the failure of BCCI was that it was incorporated in one State, Luxembourg, but had its head office in another, the United Kingdom.

*Paragraph 3: **Close links***

805. This paragraph requires the Authority to be satisfied that it can supervise an applicant or authorised person effectively, taking into account the structure of the group to which they belong, or the other firms to which they have relevant links, and the laws, regulations or administrative provisions of any non-EEA country to which they may be subject.

806. "Close links" is defined in *sub-paragraph (2)* and this sets out the structures that are relevant for these purposes. These cover the authorised person (or applicant), any parent undertaking or subsidiary undertaking of theirs and certain undertakings connected to such parent or subsidiary. In addition, the holding or control of 20 per cent of voting power by the authorised person (or applicant) in another body, or such a holding or control of voting power in the authorised person (or applicant), will constitute a close link for these purposes. These structures cover natural persons, and other forms of associations; and in such cases the relevant links are to be understood as referring to degrees of control that are equivalent.

*Paragraph 4: **Adequate resources***

807. This paragraph requires the Authority to be satisfied that the applicant has adequate resources, which has a wide meaning. The term adequate is intended to mean sufficient in terms of quantity, quality and availability, and resources is intended to include all material or financial resources, for instance capital, provisions against liabilities, holdings of or access to cash and other liquid assets. A person must also have effective means by which to manage risks. The Authority may take account of a person's membership of a group in deciding whether it is satisfied that this condition is met.

Paragraph 5: Suitability

808. This paragraph requires the Authority to be satisfied that the person is "fit and proper" to be permitted to carry on the relevant activities, taking account of connections with other persons, the range and nature of regulated activities he carries on (or proposes to carry on), and the overall need to be satisfied that his affairs are and will be soundly and prudently managed.

Part II: Authorisation

809. This Part provides that the threshold conditions set out in paragraphs 1 to 5 are relevant to any additional Part IV permissions held, or applied for, by EEA or Treaty firms. However, the conditions are not relevant to an EEA or Treaty firm's qualification for authorisation under Schedules 3 or 4.

Part III: Additional conditions

810. This Part enables the Authority to specify additional conditions for an applicant for authorisation with a head office outside the EEA and who seeks to carry on regulated activities in relation to insurance business. Paragraph 9 confers a power on the Treasury to amend the threshold conditions by order.

Schedule 7: the Authority as Competent Authority for Part Vi

Paragraph 1: General

811. This paragraph applies the provisions of the rest of the Act to the Authority, with certain modifications, when it is exercising the competent authority function. The remaining provisions of the Schedule set out what these modifications are.

Paragraph 2: The Authority's general functions

812. This paragraph disapplies the Authority's general duties under section 2 by ensuring that the definition of its general functions in section 2(4) does not include functions of the competent authority under Part VI. (Section 2(4)(b) is not mentioned since the competent authority does not have a statutory function of making codes.) However the competent authority is placed under a separate obligation, by section 73, to follow analogous principles.

Paragraph 3: Duty to consult

813. This paragraph disapplies section 8 which places a duty on the Authority to make arrangements for consulting practitioners and consumers. The competent authority already has a listing committee which it consults and which the Authority has said will continue in operation following the transfer of functions from the Stock Exchange to the Authority.

Paragraph 4: Rules

814. Under this paragraph, section 155, which relates to consultation on rules, is applied with appropriate modifications to the listing rules made by the competent authority.

Paragraph 5: Statements of policy

815. This paragraph deals with statements of policy made by the competent authority under section 93. It has the effect of requiring that when the Authority publishes such statements, it must not delegate this function, but must act through its governing body, as provided for in paragraph 5 of Schedule 1.

Paragraphs 6 and 7: Penalties and fees

816. This paragraph disapplies provisions of Schedule 1 which would otherwise apply to the imposition of penalties by the competent authority, because these matters are provided for separately in section 100. Similar provision is also made, in paragraph 17 of Schedule 1, in relation to the charging of fees for which separate provision for the competent authority is made in section 99.

Paragraph 8: Exemption from liability in damages

817. The competent authority has exemption from liability in damages under section 102 and accordingly this paragraph modifies paragraph 19 of Schedule 1 which deals with similar issues for the Authority in its general regulatory role.

Schedule 8: Transfer of Functions under Part Vi

818. The provisions of this Schedule allow the Treasury to transfer some or all of the competent authority functions to another body if it is in the public interest. Three specific grounds covering the performance of the functions and competition issues are set out in paragraph 1(2). These are particular situations in which the Treasury consider that they might exercise the power to transfer functions. The purpose of setting out these particular examples of public interest grounds in the legislation is to provide more certainty in this area. Any order the Treasury makes under this Schedule would be subject to debate in both Houses of Parliament. This is provided for in section 429(1)(b).

Schedule 9: Non-Listing Prospectuses

819. This Schedule applies the provisions of Part VI so that they apply in relation to a non-listing prospectus as they apply to listing particulars. It makes a number of changes to those provisions to deal with the fact that securities which are the subject of non-listing prospectuses are not admitted to listing.

Schedule 10: Compensation: Exemptions

820. This Schedule sets exemptions from the liability to pay compensation for false or misleading particulars in certain circumstances under section 90. Paragraph 5 provides that a person is not liable to pay compensation for loss resulting from a statement in the listing particulars which reproduces a statement made, for example, in a public official document. Paragraph 6 provides that there is also no liability if the person against whom action is taken satisfies the court that the person who acquired securities did so in the knowledge that a statement in the listing particulars was false or misleading. In such a case the person suffering the loss would not have been misled.

Schedule 11: Offers of Securities

821. In accordance with EC law requirements, section 84 requires a prospectus to be approved and published where any person offers securities to the public in the United Kingdom for the first time and when an application for listing has been made. Section 103 provides that whether securities are offered to the public in the United Kingdom is to be determined in accordance with the requirements of this Schedule. This Schedule therefore defines an offer to the public, subject to certain exemptions which are set out in accordance with derogations in EC law.

Schedule 12: Transfer Schemes: Certificates

822. The Schedule sets out the details of the certificates which the court must be satisfied, under section 111(2)(a), have been obtained.

823. Part I deals with insurance business transfers. The certificate requirements are all necessary to implement the insurance directives. For all insurance business transfers, a solvency margin certificate is required under paragraph 2. This certifies that the transferee has the necessary margin of solvency (defined in sub-paragraph 2(4)). It must be issued by the home State regulator in the case of an EEA firm under Schedule 3, the Swiss supervisory authorities in the case of a Swiss insurance company, and the Authority in all other cases.

824. If the transfer concerns a UK authorised person authorised under the insurance directives and the business to be transferred is conducted from a branch in another member State, a certificate is needed under paragraph 3 to the effect that the host State regulator has been duly notified and has responded (or the 3 month period allowed for response under the directives has elapsed).

825. If the transfer is of business which relates to the effecting and carrying out of long-term insurance (other than reinsurance policies) involving policyholders from other member States, and it involves a UK authorised person authorised under the First Life Directive, then a certificate is needed under paragraph 4 to the effect that the relevant authorities for those other member States have been duly notified and have consented (or the 3 month period allowed for response under the directives has elapsed).

826. If the transfer concerns a UK authorised person authorised under the First Non-Life Directive, and the business to be transferred is business which relates to the effecting and carrying out of contracts of general insurance which includes policies (other than reinsurance policies) concerning risks arising in other member States, a certificate is needed under paragraph 5 to the effect that the relevant authorities for those other member States have been duly notified and have consented (or the 3 month period allowed for response under the directives has elapsed).

827. Part II deals with banking business transfers. All such transfers require a financial resources certificate under paragraph 8. This certifies that the transferee has or will have adequate financial resources. It must be issued by the "relevant authority". In a case where the transferee is a person authorised under Part IV or Schedule 4, this is the Authority. Where the transferee is an EEA firm under Schedule 3 it is the home State regulator. Where the transferee is neither, it is the relevant authority in the place in which the transferee has its head office.

828. If either the transferor or transferee is an EEA firm under Schedule 3, a certificate is also required under paragraph 9 to the effect that the home State regulator has been duly notified and has responded (or the 3 month period allowed for response under that paragraph has elapsed).

Schedule 13: ***the Financial Services and Markets Tribunal***

829. This Schedule makes provision further to that contained in Part IX as to the constitution and operation of the Tribunal.

Paragraph 2: ***President***

830. This paragraph requires the Lord Chancellor to select one of the members of the panel of chairmen, with qualifications as specified in paragraph 2(5), to be the President of the Tribunal. Apart from his general responsibility for the Tribunal's functions under paragraph 2, it is the President's responsibility under paragraph 7 to establish standing arrangements for the selection of panel members to sit on the Tribunal to hear particular cases. The standing arrangements must provide for the selection of at least one member of the panel of chairmen in each reference to the Tribunal, but may in addition provide for the selection other members of either panel. The Tribunal is empowered to appoint experts to assist it where necessary under paragraph 7(4). Paragraph 2 gives the Lord Chancellor the power to appoint a Deputy President, in addition to a President. If appointed, the Deputy President is to have such functions in relation to the Tribunal as

the President may assign to him, and he is able to exercise any function of the President where the President is absent or otherwise unable to act.

Paragraph 3: ***Panels***

831. This paragraph requires the Lord Chancellor to appoint the members of two panels, defined in paragraph 1 as the "panel of chairmen" and the "lay panel", from which members of the Tribunal for a particular case will be drawn. Members of the former must have appropriate legal qualifications as specified in paragraph 3(2), at least one being suitably qualified in Scotland.

Paragraph 4: ***Terms of office***

832. This paragraph provides that the terms of office of the panel members (including the President and any Deputy President) are to be determined by the terms on which they are appointed by the Lord Chancellor. The Lord Chancellor is also to have the power to remove them on grounds of incapacity or misbehaviour. The President and panel members may resign at any time, and they may be reappointed at the end of their terms. Paragraph 5 gives the Lord Chancellor similar powers to determine the remuneration of such persons and gives the Lord Chancellor the power to retain and pay administrative staff to support the Tribunal and to meet other expenses.

Paragraphs 8 to 10: ***Sittings and procedure***

833. This paragraph indicates some of the matters concerning the conduct of cases referred which may be determined by rules made by the Lord Chancellor under section 132. As section 132(4) provides, this list does not limit the Lord Chancellor's powers. Under paragraph 8, the Tribunal must sit at such times and in such places as the Lord Chancellor may direct. Paragraph 10 enables the President of the Tribunal to give directions as to the practices and procedures to be followed by the Tribunal.

Paragraph 11: ***Evidence***

834. This paragraph sets out the powers of the Tribunal to require people to attend and give evidence, or produce documents, and makes it a criminal offence not to comply without reasonable excuse. The statutory maximum fine for which a person can be liable on summary conviction is currently £5,000.

Paragraph 12: ***Decisions of Tribunal***

835. Under this paragraph the Tribunal may reach a decision unanimously or by majority, but must indicate which was the case in the document which it is obliged to issue setting out its decision. This document must include a statement of its reasons, and a copy must be sent to each party to the reference.

Paragraph 13: ***Costs***

836. The Tribunal will have discretion under paragraph 13 to award costs against any party to its proceedings where the Tribunal considered that the party concerned had acted vexatiously, frivolously or unreasonably. It will also have specific power to award costs against the Authority where it considers the Authority's decision was unreasonable.

Schedule 14: ***Role of the Competition Commission***

837. This schedule is concerned with the role of the Commission. It is introduced by section 162.

Paragraph 1: ***Provision of information by Treasury***

838. This paragraph provides that the Treasury may give information and assistance to the Commission on matters falling within the investigation. For example, the Treasury may wish to tell the Commission about its view of the UK's international obligations in a particular area, or gives its view of the systemic risk implications of changing regulating provisions or practices.

Paragraph 2: ***Consideration of matters arising on a report***

839. This paragraph provides that the Commission has to have regard to any cost-benefit analysis produced by the Authority on the regulating provisions or practices in question and to any representations made by other persons with a substantial interest.

Paragraph 3: ***Applied provisions***

840. This paragraph applies provisions of the Fair Trading Act 1973 and other competition legislation which give the Commission powers to investigate and which make it an offence to provide false or misleading information to the Commission.

Paragraph 4: ***Publication of reports***

841. This paragraph concerns the publication of reports by the Commission. When it publishes a report the Commission, like the DGFT under section 160, must so far as is practicable exclude any matter which relates to the affairs of a person which might seriously prejudice that person's interests. *Sub-paragraph (4)* provides that such information does not need to be excluded from the version of the report which is required to be sent to the Director, the Treasury and the Authority under section 162(10).

Schedule 15: ***Information and Investigations: Connected Persons***

842. Under section 165(7) the Authority may require information or documents from a person who is connected with an authorised person, including, in addition to those listed in the section itself, the persons related to an authorised person in any of the ways set out in this Schedule. These are:

- employees and agents of the authorised person;
- officers and managers if the authorised person is a body corporate, unincorporated association, building society or friendly society;
- officers, managers and agents of the authorised person's parent undertakings, if the authorised person is a body corporate; and
- managers and members, if the authorised person is a partnership .

843. In a similar way, section 171(4) enables investigators appointed to undertake investigations under section 167 to require persons connected to the person under investigation to attend and answer questions or provide information or documents. Again, this includes persons related to the person under investigation in any of the ways set out above, plus persons who, at the time the investigation is concerned with, were partners, managers, employees, agents, appointed representatives, bankers, solicitors, accountants or actuaries of:

- the person being investigated;
- that person's parent undertaking or subsidiary;
- a fellow parent of a subsidiary of the person under investigation; or
- a fellow subsidiary of a parent undertaking of that person.

844. The terms "subsidiary undertaking" and "parent undertaking" are defined in section 420.

*Schedule 16: **Prohibitions and Restrictions Imposed by the Director General of Fair Trading***

845. This Schedule sets out the procedures the DGFT must follow when he exercises his powers under sections 203 and 204 to impose a prohibition or a restriction, or vary an existing restriction without the consent of the firm, on the conduct of consumer credit business by an EEA firm. This procedure follows that which applies to the exercise of comparable powers in relation to persons licensed under the CCA 1974. If the EEA firm is carrying on consumer credit business here without a licence on the basis of its passport under the single market directives then the DGFT will need to rely on the powers in sections 203 and 204 to control that business when necessary.

846. The first step is for the DGFT to inform the firm that he proposes to impose the prohibition or restriction, or vary the existing restriction, and give the reasons for this. He has to allow the firm at least 21 days to make representations, which may be made either in writing or orally.

847. The second step is for the DGFT, having taken account of any representations received, to notify the firm of his decision and send a copy of the notification to the Authority and the firm's home State regulator. If the DGFT decides to proceed with a prohibition, a new restriction or variation of an existing one, he may also direct that the firm carries into effect credit agreements made before such action came into force.

848. The firm may appeal against the DGFT's decision to the Secretary of State, under section 41 of the CCA 1974. This gives the Secretary of State discretion to dispose of such an appeal as he thinks just (including making directions about payments of costs).

*Schedule 17: **the Ombudsman Scheme***

849. This Schedule contains further details concerning the constitution and powers of the Financial Services Ombudsman Scheme.

*Paragraph 3: **Constitution***

850. This sets requirements as to the scheme operator's constitution. These include that the chairman of the scheme operator must be appointed by the Authority with the approval of the Treasury. The scheme operator must be independent of the Authority.

*Paragraph 6: **Status***

851. This confirms that the scheme operator, its staff and the ombudsmen do not exercise their functions on behalf of the Crown.

*Paragraph 7: **Annual Report***

852. The scheme operator has to publish an annual report of its activities and also a report from the Chief Ombudsman.

*Paragraph 8: **Guidance***

853. The scheme operator can disseminate appropriate information free of charge. This could include guidance on the scheme's procedures or advice on how to deal with disputes before coming to the scheme.

*Paragraph 9: **Budget***

854. In order for there to be external scrutiny of the scheme's finances, the scheme operator's budget has to be approved by the Authority.

*Paragraph 10: **Exemption from liability in damages***

855. The efficient operation of the scheme could be significantly disrupted if its actions were subject to frequent legal challenge. This paragraph provides immunity for the scheme operator and its staff from actions for damages, similar to the immunity enjoyed by the Authority.

*Paragraph 11: **Privilege***

856. This ensures that evidence produced during proceedings under the compulsory jurisdiction is protected against actions for libel or slander.

*Paragraph 13: **Authority's procedural rules***

857. This requires the Authority to make procedural rules for the operation of the compulsory jurisdiction of the scheme. In respect of rules governing how authorised persons deal with complaints, it extends the Authority's rule-making powers under Part X of the Act.

*Paragraph 14: **The scheme operator's rules***

858. This requires the scheme operator to make other procedural rules for the compulsory jurisdiction. It provides, in particular, for rules to be made which allow an ombudsman to dismiss a complaint without consideration of its merits, for example where he deems the complaint to be frivolous or vexatious, and for the early stages of the handling of a complaint, for example a conciliation stage, to be handled by a member of the scheme operator's staff other than an ombudsman.

*Paragraph 18: **Terms of reference to the scheme***

859. This provides that the scheme operator has power to set terms of reference for its voluntary jurisdiction dealing with matters for which rules may be made under the compulsory jurisdiction. The terms of reference must be approved by the Authority.

*Paragraph 19: **Delegation by and to other schemes***

860. Although the scheme is intended to cover most complaints relating to the financial services industry, there is likely to be some continued overlap with other arrangements, for example in the areas of pensions and consumer credit. The scheme would be able to agree with other schemes which body should consider complaints within the voluntary jurisdiction. The arrangements must be approved by the Authority.

*Schedule 20: **Transitional Provisions and Savings***

861. This schedule affects the provisions of the FS Act 1986 as they relate to recognition, supervision and de-recognition of SROs under that Act. The Schedule allows the Treasury by order to designate a date from which the amendments have effect for particular SROs which are recognised under the FS Act 1986.

862. The independence of the Authority and the SROs from each other is an intrinsic feature of the system established by the FS Act 1986. Under the new regime, however, the regulatory functions performed by the SROs under the previous (FS Act 1986) regime pass to the Authority and it is therefore necessary for the Authority to be able to take appropriate steps in preparation for that transition. Were there any question whether transitional arrangements, by materially affecting the independence of the SROs, called into doubt the validity of their recognition, that could in turn cast doubt on the validity of the authorisation of firms authorised by virtue of their membership of an SRO. This Schedule makes clear that these questions do not arise and removes any potential for doubt as to whether the SROs could continue to be recognised when they cease to be truly independent of their regulator.

COMMENCEMENT

863. Certain provisions of the Act commence at Royal Assent. They are set out in section 431(1). Other provisions will be brought into force by commencement order in due course.

HANSARD REFERENCES

864. The following table sets out the dates and Hansard references for each stage of this Act's passage through Parliament.

Stage	***Date***	***Hansard reference***
House of Commons		
Introduction	17 June 1999	
Second reading	28 June 1999	Vol 334 Col2 34-111
Committee	6 July to 9 December 1999	Standing Committee A
Suspension motion	25 October 1999	Vol 336 Col 706-737
Reintroduction	18 November 1999	
Report and third reading	27 January and 1 February 2000	Vol 343 cols 594-677 and 924-1016
House of Lords		
Introduction	10 February 2000	
Second reading	21 February 2000	Vol 610 Col 13-94
Committee	16, 20, 21, 27 and 30 March 2000	Vol 610 Cols 1684-1751 and 1769 to 1804. Vol 611 Cols 9-81, 88-134, 146-233, 249-264, 503-512, 526-576, 593-632, 912-981 and 997-1059
Report	13 and 18 April and 9 May 2000	Vol 612 291-354, 561-639, 656-696, 1373-1387, 1396-1443 and 1457-1562
Third reading	18 May 2000	Vol 613 Col 363-448
Commons' consideration of Lords' amendments	5 June 2000	Vol 351 Col 38-133
Lords' consideration of Commons' amendments	12 June 2000	Vol 613 Cols 1373-1393
Royal assent	14 June 2000	

Adapted and published by GRANGIS under the OGL Licence 3.0.

www.nationalarchives.gov.uk/doc/open-government-licence/version/3/

GRANGIS - UK PUBLISHING 2022.

www.ingramcontent.com/pod-product-compliance
Lightning Source LLC
LaVergne TN
LVHW060212210926
848481LV00008B/2713